Amy Carmichael: Let the Little Children Come

by
Lois Hoadley Dick

MOODY PRESS
CHICAGO

I am as rich as a king could be;
I had a mother who read to me.

Library of Congress Cataloging in Publication Data

Dick, Lois Hoadley.
  Amy Carmichael: let the little children come

  Bibliography: p.
  1. Carmichael, Amy, 1867-1951. 2. Missionaries—
India—Biography. 3. Missionaries—Ireland—Biography.
4. Dohnavur Fellowship—History. 5. Church work with
children—India. I. Title.
  BV3269.C32D5 1984   266'.0092'4 [B]   84-16604
ISBN 0-8024-0433-2 (pbk.)

9 10 8

Printed in the United States of America

Contents

Publisher's Preface

It should be understood that this book represents a specific time frame—the opening years of the twentieth century—and that *much of what is recorded here is not true of India today.* Social reformers—British, American, Indian alike—fought to bring an end to child prostitution in India. As a result, a law was passed in 1947 making it illegal to dedicate a child to a temple.

Preface

Amy Carmichael was born December 16, 1867, in Ireland and died January 18, 1951, in Dohnavur, South India.

A biographer trying to research her life faces two drawbacks: First is the lack of personal information. Amy was so self-effacing she destroyed letters, diaries, ledger books, and even scratched out her picture in photograph albums. She never referred to herself by name in her books, either omitting all references to herself or disguising her presence by saying, "A person who was there."

The second drawback is the lack of chronological order in the limited information available. Amy's quicksilver mind and vivid imagination saw spiritual lessons in the commonplace, and she often interrupted the story of a convert to describe some beauty of nature, then forgot to finish the story. Or, while telling of a recent answer to prayer she would be reminded of how God spoke to her years ago, and the final answer to prayer she began to tell would be finished in another book!

Time became hazy to her as she immersed herself body, mind, and soul in the culture of India, becoming truly Indian. Her spirit refused to be bound by clock or calendar. In this book, we don't see Amy as much as we see *through Amy's eyes*. It is to her credit that we often lose sight of her and see, instead, her God and His doings — and the crying need of the vast Undone.

1869, England
"The horrors of the slave trade broke my heart. Anger, fear and dismay filled my heart. I could see no God, or such as I could see appeared to me an immoral God. I staggered on the verge of madness and blasphemy. I asked, Does God not care? Has God not seen? I could not love God!"

Josephine Butler

1984, New York City
"What're lookin' for? I got what yer lookin' for."
"I was thinking about eight years old—"
"You talkin' about kiddie porn?"
"Well, yeah. Yeah, that's what I mean."
"You talkin' about baby porn. Five years old?"
"Five? Yeah, that's what I mean."
"Five years old. I can get it for ya."

Overheard on a 42nd St. corner

Introduction

Black pages in history—every nation has them. What of pious Victorian England when the age of consent was twelve and little girls on their way home from Sunday school were kidnapped, drugged, crated, and shipped to houses of ill fame in South America? What of Turkey, China, and Japan? What of America in the 1980s?

In order to examine the life of one woman who daily for fifty-five years laid down her own life to save abused children, it is necessary to see her work set against its dark background. She herself said so: "The significance of this work depends upon its background—the existence, I mean, of that evil of which the lotus pool may be taken as a symbol. The waters of that pool are not clean but mirey; its depths are very deep."

It is necessary to learn certain dark facts that instead of corrupting have the opposite effect. Confronting evil in the power of God does not defile or corrupt a Christian. On the contrary, as Scripture says, evil is overcome by good.

"Little children, little children, who love their Redeemer, are the jewels, precious jewels . . ."

William Cushing

"Firmly relying ourselves on the truth of Christianity and acknowledging with gratitude the solace of religion, we disclaim alike the right or desire to impose our convictions on any of our subjects."

Proclamation of Queen Victoria,
1 November 1858

1
The Mine

1895-1897, India

She was five years old, and she wanted her mother. Light-skinned and pretty, with a mop of black curly hair, she was a high-caste child living in the temple women's house next door to the powerful bastion whose heavy carved door was the gate to hell for hundreds of little ones inside. She had enormous, perfectly round eyes like a deep-water pearl, and so she was called Pearleyes.

The temple was in a village called Perungulam, dedicated to the worship of the god Perumal. Shut away behind closed doors, Pearleyes was given picture books to look at, scenes of the vileness and depravity, and when she pushed them away the temple woman beat her soft shoulders with a stick.

But she was only five years old, and she wanted to go home to Tuticorin, twenty miles away. Watching her chance, she ran out into the street one day when the door was accidentally left open by a careless servant, but the temple woman was swiftly beside her. "*Aiyo!* Ungrateful one! Should a servant of the gods run about in the streets?"

And because it was not the first time she had disobeyed, she was dragged into the courtyard, where the woman heated an iron rod in the flame and branded her on the back of both hands.

Pearleyes lay on her mat that night, and even though another temple woman rubbed some oil on the burns, she cried. But her cry was only one in many thousands, for this was India.

India, turning the corner into the twentieth century, was little different from India through almost five thousand years of history. On the surface were colorful layers of tapestry but underneath—the mud floor and muck and dark corners and crawling things. To a new arrival, India was hot, dry air that parched the throat, filling the mouth with dust that could neither be swallowed nor coughed up.

India was a mosaic of scenes. Early morning with the sun's rays splayed out, scintillating over the marketplace, where streets teemed with noisome life, stinking of garbage, ginger, goat urine, the vendors' smoky food, incense, sweat, hot curry. A bewitchment of color. Lavish, inflammatory rug colors were set against a background of dullest squalor. Shopkeepers spilled out wares into the streets: Watery sweets speckled with flies. Ivory carvings. Leather goods and brassware. Large, practical jugs in red and blue and earth colors, mounded to stack one atop the other. Turbans purpural. Rainbowed saris hung on racks, pretty as pink tinsel. Filigreed jewelry, glass bangles, and loops of silver; golden ornaments poured out without measure on a merchant's table. Amber, the size of knuckles, strung on thong. Carnelian. Jade drops, like liquid grass.

A snake charmer with a turban as huge as last week's laundry, offering to charm poisonous snakes out of old walls, sat cross-legged before a cobra, its hood spread, the creature rising and swaying from side to side, eyes following the piping flute of its owner.

Tired, bony cows jostled against people in the streets, their eyes stupid and full of hopeless resignation. A fungus-spread of wasted beggar bodies — bodies — bodies — skeletal bodies as far as eye could see. A vast, open-air morgue.

Beyond the marketplace sprawled the factories making cotton goods, built by the British East India Company, who also traded in indigo and spices. Hundreds of thousands of Indians lived on the company land.

In the countryside and villages, the leitmotiv of early morning in India was the pungent smell of burning fuel cakes and blue smoke. And the women squatting with spread-apart knees, patting the cow dung into wagon-wheel-sized slabs, storing them in *batooras*, eye-high rooms of baked clay.

In the south were palm trees and propagated rice cultivation — slips of plants pegged down for firm growth. Short, dark little people with curly hair, descendants of ancient Dravidians, threshed grain with bullocks or plowed with a wood stick near fields of sugar cane, flocks of goats, hawks overhead.

Millions of Untouchables — the outcastes — who "were all horrible sinners in eons past, deserving now neither help nor sympathy while they work out their curse," any Indian would explain.

India's temples, carved from solid rock, served as sermons in stone for 92 percent of the population who were illiterate, keeping alive the deeds (and misdeeds) of the holy ones — thirty million or so — as centuries flowed over them. Outwardly imposing and stolid with an ugly barbaric beauty, some of them, like the tower of a temple in Madras, depicted eight hundred life-like figures, astonishing the beholder with its workmanship.

A Brahmin pathologist, educated in European universities, gave his opinion of the temples: "As evil as the ooze of the riverbanks. I myself went within them to the point where one is obliged to take off one's shoes, because of sanctity. Beyond lay the shrines, rising out of the mud, decaying food, and human filth. I would not walk in it. I said, No! But hundreds of thousands do take off their shoes, walk in it, worship, walk out, and put their shoes upon their unwashed feet. And I, a Hindu and a doctor, must bear witness to that!"

There was civilization and Hinduism in India over four thousand years ago. The Vedic writings of religious ceremonies and sacrifices are as old as the book of Genesis. At the turn of the century, India still had no common language. Languages and dialects numbered more than 850.

India has always been a country of villages, 500,000 of them. Over 250 million people, at the time, lived in villages or cities. Seventy percent of the people were farmers.

Madras was a large, very old seaport on the east coast of India in the Bay of Bengal, founded in 1639 by the East India Company. In November 1895, a discouraged, confused, and ill young Irish woman, Amy Carmichael, arrived just in time for the coolness of the rainy season, when water poured as if from sluices from a gray, low-bellied sky. Steamers and brigs, fishing boats and dhows clogged the harbor.

She was twenty-eight years old. Behind her lay a definite call to the mission field—but also a year's term of service in Japan, a breakdown, a holiday in China, a worsening of her condition, a trial at

Ceylon, then by Christmas 1894 all the way back to England right where she had started from.

The Christian Literature Society was in Madras, and Amy stayed there three weeks getting rested up with a missionary family. She then traveled to Bangalore, where a nurse friend had written that the climate and surroundings were "delightful!" On the way she picked up *dengue*, bone-break fever, appropriately named because of the aches and pains it brought and its side effect, depression.

"You look fresh as a daisy!" exclaimed the friend who met her, but Amy's temperature was 105° and in her own words she felt "wormy."

She knew very little of India and certainly nothing of children like Pearleyes. No one knew. The first thing she would learn—and quickly—as the Reverend Thomas Walker predicted, was that India was Satan's chosen battleground.

Amy was put to bed, dosed, cozied, and a week later felt well enough to stand on her feet again. She scrutinized herself in the bedroom mirror. A longish, oval face with a proper, straight British nose, dark wavy hair swept up behind her ears in a coil, eyes—not Irish blue like her mother's—but dark brown. Charcoal strokes for eyebrows. A controlled, rather prim mouth with all the laughter bottled up in her eyes. She wore a high-necked, long-sleeved starched dress as did the other women.

"It has been uphill work even to live," confided a veteran missionary. "The devil fights against every ray of light."

His wife added a plaintive sigh. "I feel of no use here."

There are few languages more difficult to learn

than Tamil, but Amy pitched in, and the long hours passed in language study. The sticky warmth crawled over her like a web, hugging her close, securing her uncomfortably in a mesh of heat. Her sweaty dress clung fast to her, stuck to her wet skin, and began to itch. Hours pulled out like hot, stretched taffy into weeks, months. The perplexities of Tamil conjugation knotted her brain.

Thoughts she did not like to admit as her own materialized before her: "I am too sensitive for this type of work—the weather is too wearing on me."

And one day, as she leaned her aching head on her sweaty palm: "How much more you might have done for God at home!" She recognized *that* remark as "the insinuating hiss of the enemy."

She felt tempted to laziness and remembered the Indian proverb she had translated in one of her lessons: "It is better to sit than to walk, to lie down than to sit, to sleep than to wake, and death is the best of all." Too much introspection made her morbid. She had headaches and neuralgia.

Mosquitoes and flies persisted in their friendliness. Sometimes she indulged in self-pity and injured pride. After all, she had worked for over a year in Japan, preaching through an interpreter, saw souls saved and men delivered from demons after she prayed.

The Christian church in Bangalore was very active. Active in the sense that the Christians attended church, received the sacraments, and paid their dues. Indians did love meetings! Meetings of any kind! They obligingly flocked to meetings that lasted for hours, then returned home—unchanged. The fact that there had not been one convert in a year's time did not seem to bother the Christians.

It bothered Amy. She suffered through "social times" with the other missionaries where the ladies embroidered and listened to a lecture being read. When the church pillars did take time for recreation, they associated only with each other, never including Indians in the friendship.

She discovered to her horror that unconverted Muslims and Hindus were hired to teach in the mission's school, people who could not possibly be living, daily examples of Christianity.

Depression, like a black hand, dragged her down. But, worst of all, as she described it, "The temptation to ambition—then the spiritual perishes."

One day, after letters from home arrived, Amy clutched them to her breast and hesitated on the threshold of the missionary's sitting room, longing to share them with someone. Suddenly she turned as the quick tears filled her eyes, ran to her room, locked the door, and fell on her knees by her bed, overpowered with loneliness. "How can I go on—how can I stand it all the way to the end?" She wept before the Lord.

And chilling words spoken before, which had completely astonished her, rose up again: "You don't mean to say that you think all missionaries love one another?"

A verse committed to memory, chosen by the Holy Spirit, floated uppermost among the many verses: "He that trusteth in Me shall never be desolate."

"Make Him your chief Friend and Lover," she advised a fellow worker long after that, when the Dohnavur Fellowship was a growing family.

From that day on, she shut herself in her room whenever letters came, spread them out on the table, and read them aloud to the Lord. A deeper walk and talk with the living Savior began that day, and there was no separation between them to the very end.

Even after the language is learned, she discovered, and one stands alone in a city or town, a black wave of depression can sweep up, fierce temptations call, fiery darts fall on the naked soul, or—something worse—a missionary living in the pleasantness of nominal Christianity can slide back into slack content.

This was her introduction to the mission field. Amy felt like a fish out of water in Bangalore. She was fun-loving, and there were personality clashes with the other missionaries. She shocked them by asking permission to go and live with a native family in a mud hut to learn the idiom of Tamil properly.

One afternoon, bored and brain-weary from an entire day of language study, Amy ran outdoors for a romp on her pony. She spied the dignified Resident's carriage coming up the long hill to his home, the man who represented the Queen in India seated in the back. She spurred her pony and galloped for all she was worth, hair flying in the wind, skirt ruffled up dreadfully, and raced the carriage up the hill. There! She pulled up sharp—the winner!

Her brain felt so much lighter as she trotted home, she felt relaxed and almost cheerful. But the missionaries had seen. She was in disgrace.

One older, domineering saint of God took her to task with some sharp, cutting, most unfair words. Amy's hot Irish temper flared, but Someone laid a hand of control on her. "See in it a chance to die," an inner Voice said.

The words spelled release for her old nature and an opening up of spiritual progress for herself. She bore the reprimand quietly, without answering back.

Shortly after that it was suggested to her that she would better learn Tamil farther south where it was the only language spoken. She went to live with the Reverend Thomas Walker and his wife in Tinnevelly District. ("Tinnevelly" was made up of three Tamil words: religion, food, protection.) The verse Amy read early that morning was, "My Presence shall go with thee, and I will give thee rest."

Walker *Iyer* ("teacher") was a noted Tamil scholar, known for his "devastating truthfulness." The bungalow was in the village of Palamcottah on a sandy plain with palm trees all around. Tinnevelly was bounded on the west by mountains and on the east by sea. Some of the countryside was wild and lonely, filled with robbers waiting to steal the jewels from women travelers. There was no lack of tigers, snakes, poisonous spiders.

Tinnevelly District, along with the Kingdom of Travancore, filled the southern tip of India. Through the middle sprawled the Western Ghauts, a mountain range, running clear down into the India Ocean.

Each village and town had its temple with high carved towers surrounded by a high wall. In this small district alone were three thousand temples. No Christian had ever entered the center shrine of the place where the god dwelt.

The religion told of gods who came to this world to destroy evil, but in doing this they also destroyed the evildoers. They never heard of a God who had come to destroy sin and save the sinner.

17

Seven months later, Amy and the Walkers moved about three miles north to an old mission house in the small town of Pannaivilai. Amy, along with the pastor's daughter and a handful of Indian converts, traveled in and around the area as evangelists. The Indians dubbed them the "Starry Cluster," for they recognized the sincerity and light that shone forth.

The members of the band had no salary but looked to God to supply needs. Their attitude was, "How much can I do without, that I may have more to give?"

Starting out early in the morning before the heat of afternoon could reach them, Amy and her sisters in Christ crawled inside a *bandy*, a sort of covered wagon pulled by two oxen with yokes laid across their shoulders, attached to the cart. The bandy had wooden wheels, wooden axles and pins, which squeaked and rattled alarmingly, jolting them from side to side like sacks of rice. Traveling at the rate of three miles an hour, they reached a village and walked through the dirt roads trying to strike up conversation.

Amy's first appearance in a long white dress and wide straw hat caused a stir.

A startled child first saw her and shrieked, "Oh, come and see! A giant white man is here! Oh, what a terrible sight! Run, everyone!"

"It's not a white man—it wears a dress."

"It *is* a man with a lady's hat on!"

Then, as their fear subsided, with giggles and much poking and wriggling, they crowded around the monstrosity.

"Are you married?"

"Where is your family? Why have you left them to come here?"

18

"How much are you paid for doing this work?"

"Do you eat curry and rice as we do?"

It dawned upon Amy how sensible it would be to wear native dress, and at the earliest opportunity she purchased a sari and straw sandals.

The village homes were one-room huts, sometimes two, with no furniture but sleeping mats and a chest for storing grain. Roofs were mud tile or thatched with long branches of palm trees, walls of bamboo and mud, a floor either bare earth or dried cow dung.

Bathing and family laundry were done in the village tank, in a stream, or in a well. Huts were close together, forming narrow-landed openings. Surrounding the village were fields producing rice, wheat, peas, or beans. Since labor was considered degradation, only the very necessary type of work was performed.

Men wore dhotis, a loin cloth wound about the waist and passed between the legs to form loose trousers, one end sometimes thrown up over a shoulder. Women wore the graceful sari. The jewelry on ankles, wrists, chest, arms, ears, and fingers proclaimed the wealth and position of the family.

Women used to generations of seclusion and degradation, hidden away in the *ander,* an inner room with no windows, were slow to respond to the evangelists. "I used to feel like a cat on top of a wall," Amy said, so necessary was it to be careful and circumspect.

Amy caught glimpses of the slow turn of spinning wheels in the homes and the tedious work at handlooms as thread was woven into fine cloth of cotton or silk, forming carpets, rugs, shawls.

In the Christian church at Pannaivilai was an Indian deacon whose son had married a lovely nineteen-year-old girl, Ponnammal. When the son died suddenly, the girl widow was considered the cause of the calamity, such was the superstition still binding the minds of Christian in-laws. Ponnammal, who lived with them, was not allowed to comb her hair or wash, and only dirty clothes were suitable attire for a widow. She was made the household drudge. One night, in her unhappiness, she stole out of the house and stood looking down into the depths of the garden well. How easy it would be to let herself slip down into the cool water and end forever her harsh life. Something—Someone—prevented it, and she quietly went back to bed, wondering.

Her in-laws allowed her to attend church, for the sake of appearance only, and Ponnammal heard preaching that called to her heart. She gave it to the One who could heal and forgive and put some meaning into her life.

By a miracle, she was permitted to leave the home of her in-laws—of what use anyhow was such a one who caused the death of their son due to her sins in a previous reincarnation?—and she joined Amy in her work with the Starry Cluster.

Those two happy years intinerating were jewels, as Amy said, jewels that no time could dim. Of the other, smaller, more helpless jewels, owned by the temple, Amy knew nothing as yet.

India was a land of nature's jewels. Down in the crust of the earth, toward the region of fire and molten rock, descending into hell, the worker in a mine faced darkness, depth, danger, depression, death, in order to bring to the light silver from its vein, chunks of gold, gemstones.

"Satisfied—South India," Amy wrote in her Bible at this time. Her wanderings were over. India was the mine God had directed her to. Every soul was precious, but she would discover that the tiniest, most fragile jewels were those most deeply buried.

"Mining means digging into the earth for treasures that have been hidden from man since the world began. A world without sunlight . . . a world of tunnels and passageways . . . crevices . . . pits and hiding places."

A mining engineer

"So you are going to India? How romantic!"

A friend

2
The Miner

1867-1888, Ireland, England, Japan

The village of Perungulam where Pearleyes lived was just across a shallow river from Pannaivilai, where Amy lived, but Pearleyes knew nothing of this. She had decided to go home to Tuticorin twenty miles away, find her mother, throw her arms around her neck, and say, "Mother, mother, do not give me back to the temple! Oh, my own mother, keep me safe!"

She actually did walk almost twenty miles on bare, brown feet. Twice she was given a short ride in a bandy. But the temple woman followed, for no child is unwanted in India; each one is valuable to someone. The mother feared the gods, tore the child's arms from her neck, and gave her back to the temple woman.

"You are seven years old now," the evil woman said when they returned to Perungulam. "You shall be married to the god as soon as possible."

Never in her most awful dreams could the child imagine all that was meant, but she was terrified. One evening she ran across the temple courtyard and into the dark inner shrine where the ugly idol sat in a recess in the wall, a dim oil lamp flickering before him.

Bowing herself on to her face, she prayed to die. "O great and strong god, let me die!"

Seven years old, and she prayed to die.

Amy Carmichael was born December 16, 1867, in Northern Ireland, in the village of Millisle, facing the Irish Sea. She was the oldest of seven children.

The Carmichael flour mills, owned by her father, David, and her uncle William, gave employment to the people in town. Some of the mill profit helped build a school, provided night classes for employees, and sponsored evangelistic services on Sunday nights.

As a child, Amy learned to love the sounds and ever-changing colors of the sea, the flowers in the garden, all living things. In fact, she rearranged her doll house by sweeping out all the miniature furniture and little mannequins and moving in beetles, mice, moss, froglets, and pretty stones.

She was the leader in all sorts of mischief, harmless and otherwise. One day when she and her two brothers were swinging on the garden gate, Amy looked at the laburnum tree and remembered that the pods were poisonous.

"Let's see how many we can eat before we die," she said. The little boys happily agreed. The children stuffed themselves, but fortunately Mother found them in time and administered an abominable medicine guaranteed to bring up the pods.

When Amy was three years old she prayed earnestly that her brown eyes would turn to blue, her favorite color. She fell asleep confidently. Her mother had said, "God always answers prayer."

In the morning she ran to the mirror, never doubting the miracle, but the God who could see far down the years to her adventurous excursions into the underworld of India, had answered for her best good. He said no.

Born into a Christian family, growing up with a background of two-hour church services, long prayer meetings, a strict atmosphere in which only psalms were sung on Sundays, Amy developed a strong faith but also a rebellious will against any formalized religion that did not encourage a child-Father relationship with the Almighty. When she stood alone in India, especially in the early days of the Dohnavur Fellowship, her Christian life was stripped of entanglements and utterly simple — a child depending upon a heavenly Father.

Until age ten, Amy studied at home with a governess and was free to swim, ride, and visit neighbors, taking them great pots of homemade soup from her mother's kitchen. Next to the minister's house lived a missionary on furlough from India, and Amy often begged to hear stories of that land, never dreaming she would someday become a mother to almost a thousand Indian children.

Soldanella, age ten, was one of those children. She was a child-wife with a malicious mother-in-law who schemed to use the beautiful little girl to win promotion for her son. She dressed the child in light green silk, with a darker green spun with gold thread for the border of her sari, decorated her with jewels and bangles, a tiny gem by one nostril to draw attention to the delicate nose.

A carriage conveyed her, a captive bird, to the office of her husband's boss. Fearful, her heart-sounds making her feel faint and light-headed, Soldanella climbed the stairs and passed a glass window. "If he tries to touch me, I will break that window and eat the glass," she vowed.

She knew nothing of God, nor did she believe in

the old gods. A Power she had never heard of protected her that hour, and she did not eat glass.

Though only ten years old, she was an intelligent child. She knew enough to ask a lawyer how long she would have to wait before she could escape to the place called Dohnavur where they protected children.

"Six years," the lawyer said. She must resist evil, resist and resist and suffer and wait for six years. And she was only ten years old!

When Amy was eleven years old, in 1880, she was sent to a Wesleyan Methodist boarding school in Yorkshire. She began to write poems then.

She was considered a rebellious, wild, Irish girl, often in trouble with the headmistress, but "there wasn't a teacher I didn't love." A staunch Presbyterian, attending a Methodist school, later greatly influenced by her Quaker friend, Robert Wilson, helping in his Baptist Sunday school, yet appreciating the Church of England liturgy, Amy came at last to drop labels and to accept all born-again ones as part of God's family.

When Amy was thirteen a visiting speaker gave his message to the assembled girls, then asked them to bow their heads and sing "Jesus Loves Me." During the quiet minutes that followed something happened to Amy. She had always known the gospel story, but this time it was personal, and she invited the Lord Jesus into her life. Some years afterward she found words to describe her experience.

> Upon a life I did not live,
> Upon a death I did not die,

Another's life, Another's death,
I stake my whole eternity.

When her father died in 1885, the family was living in Belfast, and Amy was called upon to be her mother's companion and almost a second mother to the younger children. There was a great famine in China at the time, and Amy remembered that her mother, a widow with seven children, yearned to go as a missionary.

One rainy Sunday morning Amy and her two brothers were returning home from church when they passed an elderly woman struggling with a heavy package. On an impulse, Amy turned to help her. This meant facing all the proper church people walking in prim rows home to Sunday dinner. Eyebrows lifted and knowing looks passed across faces. Didn't this constitute *working* on Sunday?

Amy, red-faced and very embarrassed, held onto one elbow of the poor old woman and helped her carry the bundle. As she helped her across the street and up the curb, a verse came alive like a flash of light:

"Gold, silver, precious stones, wood, hay, stubble; every man's work shall be made manifest: for the day shall declare it, because it shall be revealed by fire; and the fire shall try every man's work of what sort it is. If any man's work abide . . ." (1 Corinthians 3:12-14).

She could have sworn a voice shouted the last part, "If any man's work abide," and she stopped and looked around. There was no one in the street now. But she knew something had happened that had changed her values. Nothing would ever matter again but the things that were eternal.

She was seventeen years old. That afternoon she kept to her room in prayer. After that, everyone saw the change. She threw herself into service for God, visited homes, held children's meetings, taught night school in slums, organized a morning watch of prayer and Bible reading, started a schoolgirl's prayer meeting, and volunteered at the YWCA.

In September 1886, she visited Glasgow, Scotland, and attended a deeper-life convention. The atmosphere was foggy—fog inside the auditorium, fog across the rows of people, and a bit of fog in her own heart. For months she had been struggling to live a "good" Christian life and be holy. Had she not many excellent works to recommend her?

It was all demolished in the last line of the speaker's prayer, the only part she remembered: "Now unto Him Who is able to keep us from falling" (Jude 24). *He* does the keeping! He keeps from *falling!*

She and her friend dined in a restaurant, and the mutton chops were served quite rare. Her friend complained. All Amy could think of was, "He is able to keep us from falling!"

Back home in Belfast, the time of mourning and wearing black for her father was over, and her mother took her shopping for new clothes and party dresses. Amy needed clothes, but—party dresses? She shook her head. Life was short, and she didn't want to waste any of it.

In Belfast there lived thousands of girls and women who worked in factories and were nicknamed "shawlies" since they could not afford coats or hats but bundled up in big plaid shawls through all kinds of weather.

"Go to church? Who, me? And what'd the smart toffs say if they found a 'shawlie' in their seat?"

Amy paid a visit to the minister of Rosemary Street Presbyterian Church and asked permission to hold a meeting for shawlies only. It was a daring, new idea, but he agreed.

"That Amy Carmichael is a headstrong one, she is," the church folks said. "Those dirty, rough mill girls weren't made for church-going. They wouldn't understand sermons or hymns." And the officials of the church were most uneasy over the very thought of such goings-on.

Amy had already been visiting in the slums and made friends with the girls. Her brother Ernest worked in a railroad shop in that very area and told her the details of crime and poverty the shawlies had to face.

Amy led the shawlies' church service, and it grew until it overflowed the church, and she realized they needed a hall that would seat at least 500. An iron hall could be erected for 500 pounds provided they had a piece of land to put it on. They had neither money nor land. Amy visited a businessman, one of the biggest mill owners, and asked the price of his land. He gladly gave the land, charging a token yearly rental sum of less than one dollar.

"Shall we ask the minister to take a special offering for the money to buy the hall?" asked one of Amy's co-workers. "There are many wealthy people in the church who could give that amount and never miss it."

Amy thought it over, then said, "Don't you think God could make His own people *want* to give without being asked? The Bible tells us to ask *Him*, and not to beg. It would be safer just to pray. If he answers, we will know it is His will to build the hall."

No one had set a precedent for Amy. She had never heard of anyone who secretly prayed for money and received it. With her friends she prayed every day, kneeling in a church pew, while one elder stood in the doorway, keeping an anxious eye on "that Carmichael girl" and her queer escapades.

Shortly after, Amy was invited to dine with a Miss Kate Mitchell, whom she had never met. Miss Mitchell wanted to hear all about the shawlies and Amy's work. Two days later, Amy received the 500 pounds for the hall from the lady. "The Welcome" hall was built and dedicated, and evangelistic services begun by two of D. L. Moody's students.

"That in all things He may have the preeminence" was the motto hanging on the front wall. Every night souls were saved. "The Welcome" was open seven days a week as Amy planned services, sewing clubs, choir practice, reading lessons, and mothers' meetings for the girls.

When Amy was twenty-one she was asked to begin another mission work in Ancoats, Manchester, among factory girls. Since "The Welcome" was thriving under the leadership of Miss Mitchell, Amy agreed. Her mother accompanied her and took a position as lady superintendent of a rescue mission. All the money left by Amy's father had been lost. Amy herself rented a room in the slums, a filthy room crawling with little creatures. Her meals were oranges and tomatoes eaten while reading a book to save time.

One night a gang of men followed her, surrounded her, and she was saved from being molested by a woman who ran out from her home and dragged Amy inside. But the front door hung on a broken hinge, and only a white sheet hastily hung in the doorway stood between Amy and danger.

Only a sheet! It might well have been a stone wall thirty feet thick, for Amy enjoyed divine protection.

God had given Amy a pattern upon which to build a Christian work, as she studied the book of Ezra.

"The adversaries . . . said, Let us build with you" (Ezra 4:1-2).

"We ourselves together will build" (Ezra 4:3).

"Then ceased the work of the house of God" (Ezra 4:24).

Later, "Who commanded you to build this house?" (Ezra 5:9).

"We are the servants of the God of heaven and earth" (Ezra 5:11).

"Let the house be builded . . ." (Ezra 6:3).

"And let the expenses be given out of the king's house" (Ezra 6:4).

"Unpractical!" was the cry of many of God's people to this type of building, but Amy held fast to the pattern to the end of her life.

"It is enough to ask the Father only for money for His work." And she added that only those determined to build in gold, silver, and precious stones should be allowed to help.

Amy plunged right into the mission work in Ancoats, but she learned a hard lesson that caused her to write in later years, "The secret of going on is getting away." She skimped on sleep and nourishing food, and finally her health broke down, and she was obliged to give up all work.

Just at this time, a sixty-year-old Christian gentleman, Robert Wilson, whose wife and only daughter had died, invited Amy to Broughton Grange for a rest. He was one of the founders of the Keswick Convention and a speaker at such meetings. Broughton Grange was a chosen school, Amy said, in which great spiritual lessons were to be learned before she could be used as God planned.

She learned to "be a deep well, a deep well doesn't talk," since she took care of Mr. Wilson's correspondence and knew the secrets and problems of many people. Listening to his teaching, she learned how to illustrate a talk with a vivid anecdote. She learned to live under disapproval and remain quiet, since Mr. Wilson's sons did not welcome her at Broughton Grange.

During this time D. L. Moody spoke at the Keswick Convention, and afterward he and Mr. Wilson strolled down the street together. Suddenly Mr. Moody stopped talking, for his voice was breaking. He repeated the text he had just preached on. "Son, thou art ever with Me, and *all that I have is thine.*"

"I never saw it before," he said. "Oh, the love! God's love!"

Tears rained down his cheeks, and Amy never forgot that spiritual truth, "All that I have is thine." It reinforced her faith that God knew her needs before she asked and wanted to supply them by faith. Not in any other way.

At Keswick she had prayed for rest from the

knowledge that thousands of souls every day died without Christ, and that God would make her glad to stay at home and send others. Not once did it occur to her that God might send *her*.

"Come over and help us" became a cry to her personally on a snowy evening in 1892. "He says *Go* — I cannot stay," she wrote to her mother. Still, she felt as though she stabbed to death the dear old man who was her second father. Amy, frail in health, subject to neuralgia and headaches, the financial support of her widowed mother who was left with seven children, the least likely to pioneer in a pagan land, was called by God. An old, oft-repeated story. God uses nobodies, foolish things, things that are nothing. For so she considered herself.

And her brave mother's reply was to go. Her heart echoed God's command.

Was it not cruel and a betrayal of trust to desert dear Mr. Wilson? Amy said nothing to the storm of misunderstanding from his relatives, but it hurt. Was this storm sent to prepare her for greater storms later? She would need the preparation.

Her own aunts misunderstood. They thought she was drawn by love of travel and adventure, yearning for a change. People in general considered it a terrible mistake.

"It will mean Mr. Wilson's death," said leaders in the Keswick movement, renowned Bible teachers, and their words tore her heart. After many years she realized that one must expect to be misjudged — *Christ* was.

In 1888 the Keswick Mission Committee was organized, and Amy was its first missionary. She had applied to the China Inland Mission, but its doctor rejected her. A year passed. The way seemed open for Japan, and Amy worked hard there but after fifteen months broke down with brain exhaustion, fever, and pain.

She tormented herself with questions: Had she made a mistake? Couldn't she have done so much more in the same time at home?

"These innocent children are made victims and are prepared for an immoral life by a course of training from their early days. The Temple and the illiterate Hindu public are responsible for developing a kind of mentality in those children which makes them, when they grow to be women, view a criminal, unholy and antisocial act . . . as a hereditary right and a caste *dharma* (duty).

> *Dr. Mutthulaksmi Reddi, lady physician of Madras, first woman to sit in an Indian Legislature*

"There are, I am sorry to say, many Temples in our midst in this country which are no better than brothels."

> *Mahatma Gandhi*, Young India, *6 October 1927*

3

The Keeper of the Jewels

Five thousand years of Hinduism

It was not safe for a girl-child to be walking alone on the road at dusk, so the kindly old woman carrying a water jar stopped, retraced her steps, and called to the child. The heavy liquid sun set in an orange glow and clouds of dusty gold. There wasn't a moment to waste.

"Child, where are you going, and who do you want?"

Pearleyes had stolen out of the temple again, down the village street, across a stream, through a grove of palm trees, and on to the next village. Surely the temple women were blind that day. On the road by a church she paused, a little lost lamb waiting to be found.

"Beware of the child-catching Missie *Ammal* [mother]," the temple woman had tried to frighten her. "She will rub a magic powder on your arm and you will have to follow her."

Could it be worse than the temple? "I have run away from the servants of the god in the temple. I am looking for the child-catching Ammal."

The woman on the road was a Christian, but she said, "Impossible. How could such a little thing as you escape from *them?*" Nevertheless she took Pearleyes home with her, just for the night. In the morning she must return her to the temple, for the woman greatly feared the priests.

Pearleyes, hungry and thirsty, refused to eat. She knew she was a high-caste child, and she went to bed hungry rather than break caste.

India had every type of religious practice — something for everyone. The number of the gods suggested infinity. One god may be represented in one thousand forms, present anywhere.

Almost every moment of the day was governed by some sort of religious ritual. Centuries of hunger, poverty, overpopulation, and war contributed to the other-worldliness of the Hindu. Hinduism welcomed all other beliefs, incorporating them into itself, rejecting nothing, thus surviving all onslaughts, refusing to be conquered.

Hinduism was bewildering, elastic, ambiguous. It shaped a mentality unlike any other in the world. Whatever one was seeking, it might be found in Hinduism. Faith or speculation. Holiness or sensuality. Rationality or irrationality. Practical or visionary. Meditation or ceaseless works. Devil worship or high-minded philosophy. Hinduism had them all.

Hinduism has a trinity: Brahma, the creator; Vishnu, the preserver; Shiva, the destroyer. These three may manifest themselves in thousands of lesser gods or objects or animal life. A god may often visit earth as an *avatar*, a holy leader. Hindus claim Krishna, Mohammed, Jesus Christ, and many others as avatars.

Hindus yearn after three main objectives: eternal life, knowledge, and joy, all of which are possible only by union with God. This union is achieved by bland resignation and submission to the endless cycle of existence, reincarnation into higher and higher forms of life finally culminating in *nirvana,* a state of nothingness.

"He has sinned in a former life, he must be cleansed by suffering," applies even to the crippled, starving beggar child. Hence, the motive for good deeds, self-denial, and flagellation is a most selfish one.

The Hindu believes in a human attempt to atone for sin by sacrifices, courage, and patient acceptance of whatever life he is in. Doctrine may be invented to accommodate or justify any rationalization. *Karma* is the law of cause and effect in reincarnation, the belief that every person is accountable for his earthly deeds. Those deeds determine if he will be reborn as an insect, an animal, or in a lower caste, or higher caste, on his way toward nirvana.

Hindus accept without complaining dirt, hunger, and any suffering, since it is to prepare them for a better life in the next reincarnation. *Dharma* is the code of duty to keep caste.

To a Hindu, the entire world is considered an illusion. Thus it follows that an embarrassing or painful condition may be declared not to exist.

Hinduism is fatalistic, believing that even if the world progresses and becomes better, the universe dies periodically and is reborn, to repeat all previous existences. Therefore one should endure the present life and do good deeds to ensure a higher one next time.

The illiterate of the population bow down to idols already made or create their own with sticks and stones, and worship by means of festivals and parades. Others believe in a supreme God, Brahma, and consider all idols but his representatives, necessary for the uncomprehending lower classes.

The Ganges is considered a river of salvation. If one bathes in its waters he is released from caste and sin and will be reborn into a higher caste.

"A Hindu must not take life, not even put an end to hopeless animal pain," explains one text. The cow, especially, represents all the gods combined and is equal to a high-caste Brahmin. It is a greater sin to kill a cow than to kill a man. (An estimated 230 million cows wander the streets of India, starving, diseased, suffering thirst. If injured, they are left to die.) In unexplainable contrast, it is permitted to inflict pain upon animals. A bull pulling a cart may have his tail twisted until the bones break to make him hurry.

A Hindu man fears his soul may enter hell unless he leaves sons behind him to pray for his speedy reincarnation. Only a son can perform the funeral ritual so the father may possibly have a brief stay in heaven. "Sons, many sons," is the prayer of the devout Hindu.

Caste (the word means *color)* began when the Aryan invaders in the year 2000 B.C. conquered India's black aborigines and dark-skinned Dravidians. Since the deity determines caste, to break caste is a great sin.

The temples, thousands upon ten thousands all over India, sometimes carved from one solid mountain of rock, were fabulously wealthy, yet the concept of charity did not exist. The temples never gave to anyone; they took only. Idols and shrines were everywhere.

Amy Carmichael described one scene of worship. The Hindu crouched over a pond or stream or place of water which represented to him the sacred Ganges. He bathed, then marked his fore-head, arms, or breast with his cult signs. Tying up his hair, he scooped up water in the right hand and poured it into his mouth for inner purification, calling upon his particular god.

Then, the regulation of the breath: The right nostril was clamped shut with the thumb, snorting out the breath through the left nostril. Then the order was reversed. Then the nose was pinched shut completely to prepare the soul for prayer.

Facing the east, the man said, "Let us meditate on that excellent glory of the Vivifying Sun, may he enlighten our understanding."

The second part of the ritual began. The man, praying for vigor and strength, sprinkled water on his head for cleansing of all guilt. Just as the keen flashing line of the sun rose above the horizon the man threw a handful of water into the air toward the east.

His left hand, hidden under his belt, counted upon a rosary 108 repetitions of a prayer. Next, an invocation to Mitra, the ancient god of the Persians. The man then named all his ancestors, calling upon the god of gods, the Supreme Lord of the universe. He ended by sipping water for the cleansing of his soul.

"But do you feel forgiven? Are your sins really gone?"

"Sin, what is sin? A word, a breath, delusion. How can I sin, I not being I, but Brahma?"

The goddess Kali stood upon the body of a child, her own black tongue lolling out, wearing a necklace of the skulls of children, a headdress of snakes, holding a bloody severed human head, and brandishing a bloody sword. Kali demanded blood sacrifices. Kali was the wife of Shiva, cruel and revengeful. Because she was most feared, she was most worshiped.

A caste of murderous stranglers called Thugs were once devoted to Kali. Their young sons learned in the home how to throw a kerchief around a neck and slowly suffocate a person. Every year thousands of human beings were thus sacrificed to Kali in the name of religion.

Hinduism contained nothing of making men better; it told only of making peace with angry gods. Indian morality was the caste system with its mighty taboos.

In Tinnevelly District stood a stone devil holding a pitchfork in one hand and a small child whom he is about to devour in the other hand. The multitude of gods all had one thing in common—ugliness.

Ordinary, everyday scenes of animist worship were dark and repellent. "*Main bookhi hun!* I am hungry!" was the cry of Kali. An outcaste Indian stood by the shrine where kid goats were sacrificed and tore the throat of a living goat with his teeth. Throwing it atop the heap of bodies on one side he seized the next kid—on and on, a practice abhorrent to orthodox Hindus, who do not take life.

Gods that must be propitiated in such a way could only appear as objects of dread. "Kali worship in the Temple was a nightmare more horrible than anything the perverted imagination of the Marquis de Sade could devise," said Lieutenant-General Sir George MacMunn writing in *The Underworld of India*.

But what of the jewels and their keepers? The Indian Census Report of 1901: "The *dev-*

adasi—servants of the gods—who subsist by dancing and music, and the practice of the oldest profession in the world, are partly recruited by admissions and even purchases from other classes. The daughters of the caste who are brought up to follow the caste profession are carefully taught dancing and singing and the art of dressing well. Their success in keeping up their clientele is largely due to the contrast they present to the ordinary Hindu housewife whose ideas are bounded by the day's dinners and babies."

Sacred postitution was common in the Middle East. The devadasis as a caste began in the ninth and tenth centuries, when most of the temples in South India were built.

Abbe Dubois, writing in the late 1700s, said the devadasis were originally for the exclusive use of the Brahmans, but in Dubois's day they received such a small salary they were forced to sell themselves on the streets.

In 1870, a Dr. Shortt wrote a paper on the devadasis, certifying that children of age five were used, and children were often kidnapped.

In 1892, a man named Fawcett wrote an article in the Anthropological Society of Bombay's *Journal* describing children dedicated to a god even before their birth.

"Sacredness with allurements, religion with lust, art with sensuousness, have combined," wrote Santosh Chatterjee in an old book, *Devadasi*.

"Thousands of young innocent children are condemned to a life of immorality and vice, of suffering and disease and finally of death resulting from infections and venereal diseases contracted in the pursuit of their profession as Hindu religious pros-

43

titutes," wrote Dr. M. Reddi.

The duties of the temple girls were to carry the *kumbarti* (the sacred light); to fan the idol with *chamaras* (fans); to dance and sing before the god. They were the only women who could read and write, play an instrument, and sing and dance. Their presence was believed to bring good luck to a wedding, and they had power to avert the "evil eye."

Indian dancing was a form of storytelling, religious in nature. The position of hands, arms, fingers, the flick of a finger or the subtle movements of eyes, all were significant to the watcher.

Indian music is hypnotic. Tight, tense little taps on a drum, then faster, doubling each drum beat, tripling each thrum, harder and faster. A dancer begins to tap her foot to the rhythm, then her hips sway, her hands undulate until, leaping into the center like an uncoiling spring, she and the drum merge and are one. Today the classical dances of the devadasis are performed as entertainment on stages of the world.

The animist devil dance, however, is a form of spiritism. "I served my god faithfully, I whirled in the dance until he possessed me and then I spoke his words," said a devil dancer in Pannaivilai.

Fiddles, wooden flutes, cymbals, gongs, horns, bells, and conch shells are part of the musical background. Through dance and music an Indian searches for one of the gods, worships him, seeks to be united with him. Symbolism gives a hidden meaning to every movement of the body. "The music is a discipline to attune one to the cosmic content of the universe."

A converted temple woman confirmed the

rumors of a secret underground traffic in children. The child, age eight or nine, was dressed like a bride and taken with another girl of the same community dressed like a boy in the garb of a bridegroom. They both went to the temple to worship the idol. The girl sat facing the god, and the priest gave her flowers and a sandal. He recited mantras and lighted the sacred fire.

The *tali*—marriage symbol—was hidden in a garland. The tali was a necklace of black beads with a golden disc hanging from it. The garland was put over the idol, after which it was put around the girl's neck. She was now married to the god, without her knowledge, knowing nothing of the implications.

The one who was to dance before the gods was given to the life when very young, otherwise she could not be trained properly. Many babies were given to temple women because it was very meritorious to give a child to the gods. If the child was old enough to miss her mother, she was very carefully watched until she had forgotten her. Sometimes she was shut up in the back part of the temple house and punished if she ran out into the street. Sometimes a child was branded with a hot iron under the arm where it did not show. Sometimes she got just a whipping.

She was taught to read and learn a great deal of poetry, which was almost entirely debased. The child's mind was familiarized with sin, and before she knew how to refuse the evil and choose the good, the instinct that would have been her guide was perverted, until the mind was incapable of choice.

"No respectable person would dedicate his

young girl or child to a temple and throw her to the tender mercies of regular prostitutes or put her in such an unfavorable, loathsome environment, except with the object of seeing her turn out as a prostitute," wrote Sir Maneckji Tadabhoy (Council of State Debates, Simla, September 1927, p. 1138).

Every temple had a *garbha-griha*—a womb house—where an idol stood, representing the god, and behind the god the power of Satan.

Walker *Iyer* described worship called *"Swami tharisanam"*—the vision of God. In the temple the priests anointed the idol with oil, decked him with flowers, burned incense, and presented offerings. The worshipers watched with empty hearts, without sense of sin or seeking of salvation.

The priest wore only a cloth around his waist and a silver cap on his head. He was hefted up to the shoulders of two men and a cup of goat blood handed up to him. Each time he drained the cup, and the mob bowed in reverence before him, howling and chanting. The stench, the noise and heat, and the feeling of evil were unbearable. And this was the "vision of God."

Gods were assumed to sleep at night, and they must be awakened by a bath, dressed, offered food, decorated with flowers. "Ten thousand people gathered at the river to wash a piece of wood," William Carey had written in dismay years before. Sometimes the god took a nap, and ceremonies before and after the nap were performed. The ceremony of awakening was called *prabodha*.

This was the environment for countless thousands of little children in India. Amy Carmichael, still not knowing of those children, faced the deadness and corruption of the Christian church; the power of Hinduism, caste and customs; the enervating climate; and the lack of sympathy from Christians in both India and Britain.

She was to learn that conversion in India meant not only an *acceptance* of Christ but a *renouncing* of all things Hindu. And the renouncing was the crucifying part.

"The dark places of the earth are full of the habitations of cruelty."

Psalm 74:20

"Unto the damsel thou shalt do nothing. . . . there was none to save her."

Deuteronomy 22:26-27

4
The Search for the Jewels

1901-1904, India

"I am Pearleyes. I have run away and come to you, and I will stay with you forever. The servants of the gods don't love me. My own mother doesn't love me. Nobody loves me!" With this disarming announcement the child climbed into Amy's lap, twined her arms around Amy's neck, and laid her curly head on her shoulder.

Amy hugged her, astonishment written all over her face. "Who is she?" she asked the woman who lingered in the background. Late the night before, Amy had arrived home after visiting a village some distance away. That very moment she was having breakfast on the veranda of the house where she lived with the Walkers.

The woman told the story. "I thought you were away traveling. If I did not see you this morning I would have taken her back to the temple."

"I was looking for the child-catching Ammal," Pearleyes confided.

The woman was greatly embarrassed. "The people call you that because children just naturally love you and follow you."

Amy laughed. She understood. She leaned over and reached to the floor for an old rag doll for the little girl.

The old woman turned and shuffled away. "It is good you came back," she called over her shoulder. "An evil place is the temple."

Pearleyes talked freely as she played with the doll. She told Amy things they did to her in the temple that blotted out the sun and made the bright day turn black. She demonstrated, using the doll.

The date was March 7, 1901. Amy never forgot that date, nor the child's story. It was terrible beyond imagination. Amy took Pearleyes to Walker *Iyer*, who questioned her, then consulted the local Christian pastor. He sent a message to Perungulam to see if the story was true. The messenger returned and reported the village was alive with temple women searching for the child. They followed. Even as he spoke to Walker *Iyer*, six women ran toward the house, hardened hags with haughty faces, expensive saris, many jewels.

"Who are you?" Walker *Iyer* stepped forward.

"Servants of the gods," said the leader.

"Shush!" The second woman nudged her. "You shouldn't have told him!"

They demanded to see Pearleyes. Amy brought her out of the house but held her hand tightly. A large crowd gathered, and there were cries of "Kidnapper! Stealer of little ones!"

A woman with bold, cruel eyes spoke up. "If you want to stay here," she pointed to Pearleyes, "you must say so yourself, so all will hear you. Or else, come back with us."

"I won't! I won't!" cried Pearleyes, almost convulsed with fear and clinging to Amy.

"She stole money from us, the little thief!"

"How much money?"

"Four *annas.*"

Amy paid the sum to the woman.

50

"Your mother gave you to the gods," insisted one. "We shall write to her."

Pearleyes hid her face in Amy's gown and shook her head. After much grumbling and threatening the crowd finally lost interest and drifted off, and the temple women left. To Amy's surprise, no one ever again even inquired after Pearleyes. She was nicknamed "Elf," and she called Amy *Amma*, the Tamil word for "mother."

After traveling each day as usual with the Starry Cluster, Amy returned home to a loving, lively welcome from little Pearleyes. There had been an empty space that her work had never filled. But if the things Pearleyes said were true, something must be done about it.

How to find out the facts? To ask questions was to close the door. India was a land of secrets. It was to be a three-year search before Amy would find out from what source the temple procured infants and children.

Still, she tried. She began by writing to other missionaries. No one knew anything. Some hinted she was imagining things. Members of the Indian Civil Service knew something but could not prove it. One of the cardinal principles of British rule in India was "religious neutrality."

Pearleyes continued to describe temple life in the uninhibited way of a child until Amy thought she could bear no more. She wept in secret and openly kept a smiling, happy appearance for the child's sake. "It was a bitter time. Few were in sympathy. It was a closely guarded secret as to how children came to the temple houses."

Once, she and Ponnammal stayed at an inn for traveling priests and pilgrims. They sat on the floor watching a garland maker string oleander flowers. The evening lamp flickered over them and shadowed Amy's face. While Ponnammal asked careful questions, Amy listened. If a man's wife died, he would dedicate an unwanted girl baby to the temple, saving wedding expenses and the bother of hiring a nursemaid. It was their first clue—an important one.

Another time she and Ponnammal slept in a cow shed. ("The cow was away," Amy hastened to explain.) Ponnammal, her mind still clutched by caste, remembered that the Lord of glory once laid in a cow's feeding box, and she humbled herself and lay down on the manure-covered dirt floor. Through the wall they heard a quarrel going on in the house.

"Three daughters—too many! Get rid of one!"

A woman's muffled sobbing.

"Give one to the temple. Is it not a worthy deed?"

Or, if a father died, they learned, a mother might sell a daughter to the temple. "She will eat good and wear pretty clothes—and never be a widow!"

A family desperately needing rice would sell a baby to the temple. If a child fell ill, the parents would vow to give it to the gods if they would send healing.

A couple with no male heirs would give a daughter to the temple. She became a "ritual son," able to inherit property and perform the funeral ceremonies. If a couple's firstborn was a girl, they would give her with the prayer that the next born would be a son.

"Alice in Underland," Amy called herself, for

she saw much of India's lowest, hidden life as she searched for clues.

One evening, in the shadowy part of a mud veranda in a caravansery, Amy sat on the floor in Indian dress, eating with her right hand from a bowl of rice and curry. Men travelers came up the steps. Each one politely gave her the sign of greeting they gave all high caste Brahmin women. Beside her, Ponnammal laughed to herself, and Amy felt a thrill of victory. She was inside India—the real India!

A government official she spoke to told her to start collecting facts. If she could find temple children, they were the best evidence.

"This land is ruled by a Christian power," retorted Amy. "Such things ought not to be."

"It is useless to move without a body of evidence at your back," he replied.

Friends mailed Amy newspaper clippings. One, from the Madras Mail, stated: "The Conference of Hindu Social Reformers supports the movement to better the condition of unprotected children in general . . . and to protect girls and young women from being dedicated to Temples."

Another government worker made plain that reverent Hindus were violently opposed to the corrupt and degrading practices that had crept into their religion.

Such efforts to stamp out the secret traffic came to nothing. They did not even begin. Public opinion needed to rise behind existing laws in order to enforce them.

One Hindu reformer suggested that temple women be retired on allowances and at their death should not be replaced. However, that too came to naught because of the demands of the worshipers.

An Indian Christian friend who visited the second most sacred temple in India told Amy of the evil that filled the place. "I never felt the closeness and power of the devil as I felt it in that Temple."

Amy kept a running diary and in it told of visiting one village where she heard of a nine-year-old to be sold to the large temple at Tuticorin. Amy pleaded for the child. "Come back in a week," said the mother, almost convinced. Amy prayed all through that long week, then hurried back to the village. Too late! The little girl lay on the floor, drugged, and a temple woman was on her way to collect her prey.

A later entry in her diary about the same child tells us that the child was married to the god, lived for a year, then died in such distress that the one responsible ran from the house covering his ears to shut out the sound of her screams.

Scorching, scorching times in which to live! How could she stand it?

While praying one day Amy pictured the Lord Jesus Himself kneeling in prayer, loving such children far more than she did, and she was comforted, knowing she knelt beside Him.

Still, three long years were to pass before they could save a second child. And, terrible words that she wrote near the end of her life's work further delineate the power of Satan: They never once saved a child after those other hands had had her in their grasp. She never heard of a child pulled out once she was involved.

A medical missionary told Amy she had lived for some time, unknowingly, next door to a temple house in an Indian city. Night after night she was awakened by the cries of children; frightened cries, indignant cries, sharp cries of pain. She inquired in the morning and was always told the children had been punished for some naughtiness. "They are only being beaten." Later, by means of her medical work, she came upon the truth.

Amy visited a Hindu town and bumped into a child, Sellamal, who had dropped out of the mission school. "Why haven't you come to school?"

The child, drooping her head, whispered. "I am learning to dance and sing and get ready for the gods."

A group of men stood near, and Amy turned to them. "Is it right to give this little child to a life like that?"

They smiled tolerantly. "Certainly no one would call it right—but it is our custom."

A little later Sellamal was the center of the gaze of thousands of Brahmins and high-caste Hindus. Every eye in the circle was fixed upon her. The men scarcely dared to breathe lest they should miss a point of her beauty as she danced.

"But afterward," Amy confronted the mother. "What comes afterward?"

The mother shrugged, palms held up. "What know I? What care I? That is a matter for the gods."

One missionary described the dancing as an overt invitation to the men present. The seemingly innocuous motions and movements were obscene.

The whole body and facial expressions are involved in the dance, but the delicately weaving hands communicate ideas in the lengthy, complicated dance-story of the gods and their loves. Indian hands, small and supple, designed for beauty and grace. Many changing rhythmic patterns, sculptured poses, and fluid flowing footwork, subtle erotic glances, seductive movements, expressive mime.

Dance practice began at 2:30 A.M. when the little girls practiced eye movements for an hour. They sat crosslegged on the floor. *Ghee* (clarified butter) was rubbed into the eyes to lubricate them. Their fingers stretched the eyelids up to the eyebrows and all during the hour the eyes never blinked. Exercise and massage followed, then a bath and very small breakfast.

From 9:00 A.M. to noon the dance dramas were practiced. Punishment was harsh. One girl was made to stand one hour in a dance position without so much as an eyewink, so the dancing master could admire her. "I used to punish her like this often to enjoy the beautiful sight."

After a lunch the children worked again from 2:30 P.M. to 6:00 P. M. Then, a bath and *mudra* (gesture) lessons. Nine o'clock was bedtime. Even after ten years of this, the little dancer had barely scratched the surface of dance lore.

Men suffering from leprosy and other disease believed they would be healthy if they married young girls, and they were willing to pay high prices.

One widow, wishing to become ascetic and holy, entered a temple but soon fled from it. "I expected whiteness; I found blackness." She told how children who are to dance before the gods begin at an early age so their natural grace is developed, their arms and legs massaged with oil to keep them flexible. The child's mind is slowly familiarized with sin. Confused and deceived her conscience is smothered, and she is no longer capable of choice.

A "joy gift" is given to the parents by the temple, thus sealing the transaction, making sure both parties know the child is not loaned but has been sold.

All temple children were marked by wearing a small gold ornament tied around the neck but hidden under the dress.

Amy was never so thankful for her childhood "no" answer to prayer than the night she stained her hands and face with coffee, dressed in sari and set out to try and get into a temple.

"Irish—but no blue eyes?" a friend commented. "Yes, you look Indian all right. How fortunate you have brown eyes."

Amy knew a blue-eyed foreigner would have been torn to pieces should she enter a temple, but disguised she might be able to find out more about temple children. She marched right past the priests and into the outer court where it was dark with only yellow torches stuck along the walls. In a dark inner shrine was a monstrously ugly idol, the only god the people knew, surrounded by saucers of oil with burning wicks. Even though people starved everywhere in India, tons of mashed bananas were sometimes poured over an idol.

She caught sight of six chubby little Indian boys in a dark back room and started toward them, but a priest darted forward and shoved her away.

Drawing her sari more closely about her face and praying for safety, she entered another larger room where ten beautiful little girls, aged four and six, stood in a line, waiting. They were dressed in silk saris and sparkled with jewels, perfumed, and wearing flowers in their hair. Their eyes were wide with fear, and they stood as carved statues. A door opened behind them, a burst of weird music, and a priest led them in.

So it was true. There was no doubt at all in her mind. But how to convince others? She returned home, sick at heart.

She kept a traveling bag packed so that she or Ponnammal at a moment's notice, whenever they heard of a baby or child about to be given to a temple, could go immediately and try to change the mind of the parent.

She describes travel in those days: first, being thrown about in a bandy for two hours, worse than seasickness, then a four-hour wait in the brutal sun along the road hoping for a bus that would stop. Heat hitting the side of her head like a bullet. A wave of nausea and dizziness, brain and stomach colliding, as the devouring heat circled her. Surely her clothes were on fire!

Bus after bus passed, crammed with rollicking people. Finally, a ramshackle bus lurched up, and she climbed aboard and wedged herself into a space between people and crates of noisy chickens. The bus stopped once at a shrine so the priest could sprinkle Siva's ashes on a wheel that seemed to be held together by twine. Then, getting out into a deserted street in a strange town, she hunted for another bus going farther. No bus. A rough and tumble ride in another bandy, which charged triple fare since the driver saw her desperation.

Arrival at the address given, only to find the baby had already been sold to a temple woman.

"But to give them to temples is honor and glory and merit to us forever. To give them to you is dishonor and shame and demerit, so why should we give them to you?"

Among the Starry Cluster was an older woman, Devai, who devoted herself to such journeys. Often she traveled two days and nights without sleep, following up any clue, returning without the baby, resting an hour, starting out again.

The three long years passed. Everywhere, Amy discovered, temple men and women appeared right on the spot to purchase a child, almost with uncanny knowledge of the opportunity.

Finally—March 1, 1904—another shining date to remember. The very first temple baby was rescued. That is, the baby was prevented from being sold to a temple. Amy held her in her arms. The tiny thirteen-day-old mite was sent by a Christian pastor who had succeeded in taking the child from a temple woman. Pearleyes picked out a name from Revelation 21:20—Amethyst. Amy had read and explained the verse, and Pearleyes liked the sound of "Amethyst."

It was almost too good to be true—except that God is good—that by June Amy had seventeen convert children besides six babies prevented from entering the temple.

The only blot on such happiness was that Ponnammal did not understand. In rescuing a child it was necessary to repay expenses incurred by the brave rescuers. And just at this time Amy heard of a father who offered to sell his eight-year-old daughter to Amy for one hundred rupees.

Buying and selling children? Are we not as bad as they? Ponnammal thought, though she said little. But the cloud was over her. Once word spread that Amy would bid against the temple for a child—prices would go sky-high! And was it right to pay money?

Amy prayed much about it but dared not hesitate, for the sake of the child. She paid the money, then prayed for one hundred rupees to drop, as it were, from heaven. Ten days later a check arrived for the exact amount, from a person who knew nothing of the matter.

Then Ponnammal was convinced the hand of God was in the rescue of the children. The day came when she could say, "I see into the future. I see God with us. This work is of Him, whatever man may say."

"Precious jewels which they stripped off."
2 Chronicles 20:25

"The East bowed down before the blast
In patient, deep disdain;
She let the legions thunder past
And plunged in thought again."
Matthew Arnold

5
Jewels Stripped Off

1899, India

When Arulai was still living in her father's house, her uncle had a servant of lower caste who swallowed a sharp piece of chicken bone that wedged itself halfway down his throat. He could not swallow it. He could not cough it up. He could not eat nor drink. He could only suck in a little breath at a time. He starved to death after great suffering.

Arulai was surprised that anyone should concern themselves about the man. "He was of low caste," was all she said.

Caste—millions condemned to be faceless. Caste—ironbound, cold, cruel with endless ramifications. Caste—destructive, spawning meaningless gestures and acts that were only symbols.

Caste prevented any notion of brotherhood, crushed personal aspirations, and prevented even hopes or dreams. Caste closed the door on opportunity, squelching talent and ability from reaching higher. Caste permitted no moving upward into a better life. Caste was reinforced by arranged marriages. Caste had no concept of equal opportunity.

From caste sprang many other evils. Caste affected even Christians in India, keeping them apart from their fellow Christians. Even Christians considered it a crime to marry out of caste or even to break the minute subdivisions. Caste made even Christians observe lucky and unlucky days.

"Death or imbecility seems better than that shameful thing, the breaking of caste," Amy mourned.

Caste could be recognized by the cut and color of dress, the angle at which a garment was worn, a mark on the forehead, certain styles of jewels and ornaments. The boundaries of caste were fixed and immovable, a rigid system over mind and body. Not only were the intelligent and skillful held down, but no high caste men, however degraded or vicious, ever sank into a lower caste.

In the experience of Amy's co-workers, the break with custom began with jewels. All over South India, women—even Christian women—were loaded with jewelry. True, they were walking safe-deposit boxes, the idea being that there was no safe place at home for the jewels. But Indians loved jewelry. Jewelry declared to the world the wealth and status of the husband; it was the family fortune on parade.

Valuable old coins, weighty nose rings, arms covered from wrist to elbow with bracelets. Silver anklets weighing two and three pounds. Pearls—real ones—around the neck. Rubies, emeralds, coral. A peasant's wife may not have food for her family, but she would have, at the very least, rings on fingers and toes, in ears and nose, gold chains—real gold—and bracelets, all set with precious gems.

Amy was always careful not to interfere with Indian customs, but the matter was brought to a head by an Indian, a young convert, who asked Amy to take his wife and instruct her how to win souls.

Amy, Ponnammal, and the young wife were riding in a bandy with the husband walking alongside. Suddenly he said, "Take off your jewels. What does a soul-winner want with jewels?"

The startled girl handed over her jewels. Ponnammal, too, looked surprised. A few days before, as she was teaching in an outdoor meeting, a little girl had pointed to her and said, "When I grow up I will join the Starry Cluster and wear jewels like that teacher."

But a woman of India—stripped of jewels—an eyesore, a reproach—could she bear it? Ponnammal stripped off her jewels.

"It set my spirit free," she said in later years. "I had a new feeling of spiritual liberty." She had made a break with custom and the fear of what people would say.

And people did talk! Just at that time the Bible teacher, F. B. Meyer from England, who saw the jewel-laden Christian women and was disturbed, arrived for a visit. In one of his sermons he pleaded that "the whole burnt offering might be laid on the altar," and he named such things as caste, going into debt, and the wearing of mountains of jewels.

Sellamutthu, a member of the Starry Cluster, had always slept at night with one hand on the beloved necklaces. "If I had loved my Savior more, I would have loved the jewels less," she said. And she removed them.

The question was not: May a Christian wear jewelry? The question was one of incurring debt, of laying aside weights, and deliverance from fear of public opinion, since the women were all members of the traveling evangelistic group.

Night traveling by bandy became safe. Thieves and robbers would not lay in wait for unjeweled women. In fact, members of the robber caste agreed to protect them. "Only because your women are not jewelled," they said. "Otherwise, we would not do it, not for any amount of money."

The Christian church was scandalized as other women gave their jewels to be sold and the money sent to a mission in China. Some returned the jewels to their families. Ponnammal's relatives on both sides were very angry, but Ponnammal saw it as preparation to do the strange, new work of rescuing babies.

Ponnammal's in-laws waited and watched. Finally they sent for her and said triumphantly, "Do you see what your foolishness has done? You have closed the heart of the Hindus."

They could not have been more mistaken, for the devout Hindu considered piety to be a renunciation of the world and its treasures. Had not Ponnammal shown that piety? Indeed. Besides, she was a widow, so what did it matter? "There are no boundaries set to her devotion!" they exclaimed and actually respected her for her decision.

Arulai, also a member of the itinerating band, removed her jewels. For her, the decision could mean her father would reclaim her and marry her to a Hindu, for so he had threatened. "If I hear you have taken off your jewels—!"

He sent word that he would meet the bandy that evening. Arulai wrapped the jewels in a piece of cloth. The bandy stopped, and Arulai's grandfather stepped out of the darkness by the road. "Your father could not come."

"Please give him my jewels." Arulai laid the package in his hand.

They never found out what must have happened

in the spiritual world, but Arulai's father never mentioned the jewels again.

As for Amy, she was accused of "dividing the church," "sowing discord," and "teaching heresy." Many were the sermons preached against her in South Indian churches. The secular press pounced upon the subject, enlarged it, exaggerated, until all of Tinnevelly District was in an uproar. Amy continued calmly with her work, only wondering what would happen to nominal Christianity and the unconverted if more pilgrims lived like pilgrims.

Caste, custom, jewels, superstition, abysmal ignorance—all come roped together. The stripping off of jewels was only the beginning. The very brave went on to defy other customs.

Amy's Indian co-workers had discovered their individuality. They were not carbon copies. They grew in character and strength.

"In India, no woman can live without marrying. It is not their custom," said a lawyer to Arulai, trying to convince her to marry an unbeliever. W. S. Grand, who lived in India, told of a Brahmin girl who died unmarried. The family felt so disgraced they paid an Untouchable to marry the dead body.

Custom allowed the money lender to charge 40 to 50 percent interest, and a man could die leaving his unborn grandchildren in debt.

"Conform to the custom of the world, lest thou be hindered in thy service," well-meaning Christians urged. In India in those years, the tiniest detail of a woman's life was dictated by custom.

Occasionally secret belief in Christ was tolerated if only there was no open breach of custom. A widow might be allowed to live at peace at home after baptism; after all, a widow was of no value.

After Amy was settled at Dohnavur with the children, two men arrived one day asking to look around. They had been told Amy was selling the little boys to slave traders in Ceylon. Such a tour of the nursery was unwise, but something prompted Amy to let them see the children.

"I didn't believe the stories we heard of their happiness," said one of the men grudgingly. Amy held up a necklace of crystal jewels, a bright stream of sunlit gems, sent by a woman who had accepted Christ as Savior and sent her jewels for them to sell to help their work. One man lifted them in his hand, hardly believing it. He was himself an agent in the secret traffic in children in the area. Amy learned later he had sold many small boys to wealthy Muslims there and abroad.

"A woman gave her jewels to buy food for these children!" he said in admiration.

Despite their nefarious work, the men had brought Amy two little boys. The men shook their heads, refusing money Amy offered for the expense of their travel. They strode away, one saying to his companion, "God is here!"

Among the workers at Dohnavur, the folly of fashion was unknown. Such a little thing as changing from India's white to economical blue in clothing drew comments. Neither was it the custom in India for one who preached to work with his hands. The first question an Indian Christian asked when applying to do evangelistic work anywhere was, "What pay shall I get?" Amy longed and prayed for workers who would come trusting God to supply all their needs. "God didn't make you all mouth," she said to some.

It was inevitable that Christians who noticed Amy's new work would say, "It is not the custom for missionaries to mind babies." Amy and Ponnammal were both used to speaking to crowds of twenty thousand people at a time. Now, they were busy changing diapers, filling nursing bottles with milk, baby-sitting, not at all "spiritual" work. The care of children was considered degrading.

"You are not a true missionary," said one friend. "You are only a nursemaid."

There were outcries and campaigns of slander against her. Amy used to dread the mail; it brought such blistering letters. All that had gone before in the way of trouble was as nothing compared to the furor when her first book on India was published, *Things As They Are*. In it she told the truth, reticent and careful not to exaggerate, but the Christian world did not wish to know. A committee was formed in India and meetings held to try and force her from the mission field as quickly as possible.

"God give me words! Firewords to arouse a sleeping world to the fate of India's soiled children!" she cried in her book.

"Thou shalt have words, but at this cost; that thou must first be burnt, burnt by red embers from a secret fire, scorched by fierce heats and withering winds," the Lord seemed to say to her.

"A book like this will gravely injure the cause of missions," was the criticism from friends in England, but the book was reprinted twelve times.

They laid to His charge things that He knew not, Amy remembered. "Go on loving, go on praying, go on forgiving, watch for the comforts of God."

Even with her lively imagination, could Amy possibly look ahead and see that within ten years she would have two hundred children, and by the end of her life almost one thousand?

It wasn't at all likely.

We are *appointed* unto afflictions.
1 Thessalonians 3:3, italics added

Onward Christian soldiers,
Sitting on the mats;
Nice and warm and cozy
Like little pussycats.
Onward Christian soldiers,
Oh, how brave are we,
Don't we do our fighting
Very comfortably?

Amy Carmichael,
from God's Madcap

6

Jewels of Victory

1899, India

In the same village Pearleyes escaped —
Perungulam — was a Christian day school that Hindu parents permitted their children to attend
without fear of conversion. After all, they were
learning to read and write and other useful things,
and no one of their caste had *ever* been converted.
Well, yes, sixty years before, two had confessed
Christ as Savior. Nothing to worry about, really.

But the schoolmaster's wife gave a Bible to a
sixteen-year-old girl, and she believed, secretly.
She was of the goldsmith caste, whose members sit
beside small fires melting the precious metal in a
pot or curved roof tile until it is refined. The gold
is purified when the goldsmith can see his face
clearly reflected in the shining gold.

The girl's older brother still anointed her
forehead with Siva's sacred ashes, but he caught
her one day washing them off. She told him she
read the Bible and loved the Lord Jesus Christ very
much. He told the family.

The family, malevolent and close-knit, built a
blazing bonfire in the courtyard and heaped on the
wood until it was hot enough to roast an ox. "Look
long at that fire. If you ever mention Him again,
you and your Bible will be thrown into the fire."
Words rapier-keen. And he meant them. Her
father, a man with a kingly, leonine bearing,

thought the matter was closed.

The girl remembered a young friend, poisoned by arsenic because she spoke of becoming a Christian. A young widow who showed a slight interest in things Christian had vanished, and her body was later found under a wooden floor.

Another girl who publically confessed Christ in her strong caste was seized by some men, stripped, and strung up by her feet in an alley. After that, she was never seen again.

The girl woke very early toward morning as she lay beside her mother, almost sure a hand had touched her.

"Go," a voice seemed to say. She had not been outside her home in three years, but she felt she must be free to follow the Lord Jesus. Her silver anklets never even tinkled as she stepped carefully over her sleeping mother, the snoring father, the aunt and brothers. If she were caught she could be sure of beating, drugging, even murder.

She hurried down the Street of Goldsmiths and waded the stream to Pannaivilai, where Amy and the Walkers lived. How did she find the mission house through twisting narrow alleys and lanes, hidden behind a grove of palm trees?

The house was very open, with many doors and windows that didn't even close properly. A layer of dew freshened everything that morning, and deep shadows still lay against the sides of house and trees. The sky turned to gentian. The girl, later named Jewel of Victory, ran up on to the porch, clapped her hands by way of announcing her presence, and cried, "Refuge! Refuge!"

Amy took her in, listened to her story, and determined to save her. Then followed noise and confusion as all the relatives and friends descended upon the mission house like a swarm of locusts to claim the girl.

The Walkers gave their upstairs bedroom to Amy and Jewel of Victory, sleeping the rest of the time on the porch. Jewel of Victory endured long, heart-rending interviews with first her mother, then other family members, and the chief men of the village, until she was near the breaking point.

"How can you betray the one who bore you, gave you suck, carried you next to her heart! Ah, my own child, my own-of-owns, my precious child, I will die of grief! You are killing me, your mother!"

The revenue inspector was called. The chief of police was summoned. Jewel of Victory repeated over and over: "The Lord is my Light and my Salvation; whom shall I fear? The Lord is the Strength of my life, of whom shall I be afraid?"

Day and night, men of the goldsmith caste stationed themselves under her window to seize her. Walker *Iyer* nailed the shutters closed. The men came two and three at a time, until forty men surrounded the house, waiting. All day long through the blinding sun-glare they waited. Just before the brilliant, brief sunset three of them rushed at the door but were stopped dead by an invisible Power.

They tried magic. They buried charms in the yard, to the East, to the West, to the North, to the South, to draw her wayward heart home, to pull her to them as a magnet pulls. Magic dust was thrown up against her window so she would breathe in a speck of it. They tried poison, but God kept her from that fate.

After many days they withdrew and gave her

rest. They burned down the mission school and the teacher's house, and the door was shut forever to any further witness in Perungulam.

South India's Tamil poet, Krishna Pillai, was invited to the new convert's baptism on Easter Sunday 1899, and he chose for her the name Jewel of Victory.

"Karia Kartar—the Doer of Things—has accomplished this," he said.

For her own protection Jewel of Victory was sent to live in a converts' home in Palamcottah. She later married a fine Christian man.

Other new Christians did not have as easy a time of it. One girl took a stand for Christ, and her ordeal lasted ten years. Her case was taken to court by the family. Day after day, week after sweltering week dragged on, when the heat was visible in long, knee-deep waves along the dust-caked streets. She was of age. She had a right to choose. She testified this over and over.

One day she was dragged off the crowded steps of the courthouse, drugged, and married by force to a heathen. The final time she appeared in court, she was a married woman and not free to make any choices at all. Her eyes were glazed and expressionless, her spirit snuffed out. And this covered a period of ten years.

Amy was told she hadn't a chance in a million if cases regarding child custody went to court. Unfair decisions were made beforehand—bribes to the judge; witnesses who, for a few annas, would swear they saw the temple woman give birth to the child. Public opinion was always against her. The very laws of the land were against her, for what was planned constituted kidnapping.

The excitement over Jewel of Victory had barely died down when another girl from the goldsmith's caste, in the very same way, escaped to Amy.

Made bold by such escapes, still another girl came to Amy, who hid her in the tower of the village church. In the morning the people of the girl's village guessed where she was and stormed the church. Walker *Iyer* allowed only two women to see the girl. The women promised if they heard from the girl's own lips that she wanted to stay, they would be satisfied.

"I fear my aunt," the girl whispered to Amy in a voice shaky with fear. "She has power."

The girl told the women of her desire to stay and learn more of the Jesus way. The aunt moved close and rubbed the girl's arm. That was all. But something unexplainable had happened.

"I come, aunt," the girl murmured and followed the woman. Amy never saw her again.

"Never count a convert safe until he or she is safe in heaven," was a word for those days.

Once a little girl of ten, not a temple child but in moral danger, sent a message to Amy: "If I can escape to you, can you protect me from my people?"

This was a child who had heard the story of Jesus' love and had witnessed to her family.

"You will see who is stronger," they replied. "Your God or ours. Do you think your Lord Jesus can deliver you from our hands or prevent us from doing as we choose with you?"

Weakened by thirty hours without food but remembering one of the Bible stories, she said, "I am Daniel, and you are the lions."

Amy was forced to send a message in reply,

"You must not try to come to us. We cannot protect you, but Jesus is with you and will not fail you."

That night the child's family shut her up in a small room with a demon-possessed woman. Next day they hinted even worse would happen.

Amy speaks of that time: "We had to stand on the shore of a dark and boundless sea and watch that little white life, swept off by a great black wave, drift further and further out, until something from underneath caught it and sucked it down." They did not see her again.

One day Amy had a visit from little Goddess of Holy Town, chaperoned by an old woman. She was a slim, graceful girl in soft, silk sari, a long plait of hair down her back, a face like a flower. Her smile was far away. Amy had known her since she was a baby and failed to prevent her dedication to the temple. Amy pleaded with her to forsake her life, as she was old enough to choose and could come to Dohnavur if she wished and if she dared to face the storm that would follow.

She cooly said, "I cannot. I am engaged to dance before the idol through the whole night."

Her smile was sadder than tears.

Once a small child training for the temple leaned on Amy's knee and said, "But am I not learning to be as you are—a servant to God?"

Mungie was a lovable child of six. Amy talked to the grandmother in the home and pleaded for her, but the grandmother's heart was hard as the stone of the temple tower and as black as the moonless night. As Amy rose to go, the woman turned to a friend and said, "Though she heap gold on the floor as high as Mungie's neck, I would never let her go to those degraded Christians."

The passing of years means little in the East where even the poorest has plenty of time, but twelve years of prayer and waiting for a child's return were just that to Amy—twelve years. Silent years.

Amy first saw Tranquility, a gentle little girl matching her name, who stood on the edge of a small group of villagers listening to gospel preaching. The story of the love of the Lord Jesus Christ was new, and she opened her heart to Him and confessed Him before all the village.

Nothing her parents could do—not threats, switchings, or supperless bedtimes—could dampen her faith. She talked continually of joining Amy in Dohnavur, until her weary parents gave in. A very happy Tranquility moved to Dohnavur and learned more of the God of love through songs, Bible lessons, and many talks with Amy.

After her father's death she asked to visit her old home and try to lead her mother to Christ. On a sunshiny day, so clear the distant mountains seemed to lean over them, Tranquility's aunt and two brothers drove up in a bandy.

"I will be back in a week!" the child called gaily, waving her hand.

"Yes, one week," said the brother, but there was a false note in his voice.

"One week." The auntie smiled courteously.

One week became six months, and Amy was bogged down in the neverending routine of the nursery and "miscellaneous oddments." Tranquility was given up to the ministrations of a magician who made charms and potions from the bodies of firstborn babies. Tranquility was given a potion.

She turned dazed and docile and obeyed as if in a trance.

After receiving no letter or message, Amy determined to find her. She and Pearl traveled by bandy, then in a broken-down, gasping bus to the jungle village where Tranquility lived. Hot, tired, and dirty, Amy and Pearl found Tranquility, but the child did not respond to them and could barely speak.

"Will you come back with us?" Amy asked.

Tranquility turned away without answering. She might have been cellared deep in the earth, such was her aloofness.

The two women held a meeting in that wild jungle village in the evening, but they were clearly unwelcome. No words of love or kindness touched the hard hearts. They slept on a porch opening out into a street filled with yapping, fighting dogs and homeless, quarreling people.

As the women slept, Tranquility's relatives gathered in the child's room, each carrying an iron-tipped spear. They surrounded her.

"Do not go with the foreign woman," one said. "If you go we will attack them on the road at a lonely spot."

The next morning Amy again asked Tranquility to return with her, but the child only gazed in silent despair, not a shred of hope in her eyes.

Soon after, she was married to a pagan, to bind her forever to her family. Two little baby girls brightened her life, so beautiful that everyone who saw them called them "children of heaven."

They went to that place at ages two and three, but not before Tranquility had taught them to lisp the name of Jesus. As the three-year-old died, she looked up, smiled, and held out her hands. Tranquility thought, "Surely the child has seen Him and His angels, she is that joyful." And Tranquility was content that the Lord of Love should have her babies. "They could not grow up good in this hell."

Tranquility was not much more than a child when she married, certainly was a child spiritually, yet she endured those twelve years, never seeing another Christian after Amy's visit. She did have a small Bible, because to the unlearned relatives it appeared to be an English lesson book. So the written Word and the living Word nourished Tranquility's mind and spirit for twelve lonely years.

At the end of that time, a hunger and thirst for Dohnavur and the Christians there welled up in her heart, and she prayed day and night, asking that someone be sent to her. The very day she began to pray, Arulai and Frances Beathe, a coworker, felt strongly led to plan a tour of those nearby villages.

Tranquility had begun to tell her people God would send her help, that He would fulfill a dream she dreamed of returning to Dohnavur. A few weeks later a bandy rattled into town, and Tranquility rushed to it joyfully, crying, "See, my God has sent them!"

The amazed people had nothing to say, and Tranquility, wild and ragged and neglected, snatched up her small son, climbed into the bandy weeping "eye-water of bliss." She was found— safe—free—after twelve lost years.

Did Amy remember then the first time it dawned upon her that "*He* does the keeping—*He* keeps from falling?" Not only able to keep an Irish girl steeped in Christianity, living in a Christian land, surrounded by loving believers, and having all the advantages of Christian civilization; but able to keep a new, young Christian with a background of gross spiritual darkness, living in an environment she called "a hell," surrounded by all that was evil, not knowing of a single other believer.

Another child believer, Mimosa, heard of God once, then was kept by Him for twenty-four years, not knowing a verse of Scripture, never meeting a Christian or going to church, until she arrived safely at Dohnavur. Satan's victories are not victories; they are only temporary hindrances to the purpose of the Victorious One.

Deareyes, like Tranquility, was not in danger of being given to the temple. She was eight years old when her family allowed her to live at Dohnavur, and within a few years she was a trusted helper in the nursery. That year Amy was obliged to go to Madras for three days. "There are times when it is not easy to be four hundred miles away."

The girl's uncle was a magician, and he sent her a small tin box with a note telling her to rub her hand over the box. Not understanding the ways of the occult and the power of Satan, she obeyed. She fell into a trance. The uncle came to Dohnavur (where it was not unusual to see cobras) disguised as a snake charmer. Deareyes never remembered what happened, except that when she awoke she was in her sister's home in one of the border towns far from Dohnavur. A Hindu marriage had been planned for her.

Her brother threatened her with a knife. "You will marry this man, or I will kill you. And afterward, I will kill myself, for I have no desire to be hanged."

Deareyes wept and refused, finally saying, "If you find me a Christian I will marry."

A "Christian" was found, but he was only a pretend Christian, and so began a married life that could be described in the words of Jonah: "The waters compassed me about even to the soul; the depth closed me round about, the weeds were wrapped about my head. I went down to the bottom."

All that time she had no help from any human being. She was closely guarded. Only God's presence in her heart kept her from giving up. She could not get a message to Amy, and Amy heard nothing of her.

After her husband died, she determined to escape to Dohnavur with her little boy. One of the relatives agreed to take her to visit the magician uncle who lived near Dohnavur. At first he watched her carefully, then relaxed his guard, and she ran out of the house and reached Amy. After fifteen years and six months.

"Victories that are easy are cheap. Those only are worth having which come as the result of hard fighting," said H. W. Beecher, and the "hard fighting" part was Amy's very life.

Is it ever safe—or true—to write "in vain" over any work for God?

Amy found it comforting to remember that even earthly jewels are almost indestructible. Somewhere in the world are the jewels that Aaron wore when he went into the Holy Place. All are safe somewhere.

For Amy, "lost" meant "not yet found."

"A mother at nine years of age delivered by Caesarean section of a baby weighing less than two pounds."

Legislative Assembly
Debates, 1922

"The number of Hindu girls who are already widows at ten years of age or under is still over 96,000, while no fewer than 329,076 Hindu widows are fifteen years old or less."

Census of India, 1921,
vol. 1, part 2, p. 46

7
Broken Jewels

1915-1927, The years of public outcry

"So many, so young and all accursed," was the unknowing remark of a Hindu woman as she saw thirty mission girls passing by on their way to church, draped in their usual white shawls. She mistook them for widows.

Although Amy's work was not mainly directed against the evils of child-marriages, child-widows, suttee, or infanticide, she came into contact with those things many times. A book outlining her life would not be complete without mention of the child-jewels, many as young as five or six, who were broken by these customs and condemned to a life of suffering; five- and six-year-old child brides, ravished, diseased, broken in body and mind.

According to the Legislative Assembly Debates, each generation in India saw the death of 3,200,000 little mothers in the agony of child birth. It was common to marry a girl of three or four years and allow consummation when aged nine or ten.

Evidence that the above customs prevailed, especially in South India, was furnished by American, English, and Indian social reformers alike. At the same time Amy Carmichael began her work of rescuing children in danger of temple life, Katherine Mayo toured India, interviewing both British and Indians who were concerned about India's children. Both Amy and Bishop Henry Whitehead, who had lived in India forty years, twenty-three of them as Lord Bishop of the Great Indian Diocese of Madras, confirmed her findings as true.

None were more vocal and more determined to right the wrongs than the Indian people themselves.

"Is it not a sin when they call a baby of nine or ten years, or a boy of ten years, husband and wife? It is a shame! Girls of nine or ten, babies themselves who ought to be playing with their dolls rather than becoming wives, are mothers of children. Boys who ought to be getting their lessons in school are rearing a large family of half a dozen boys and girls," stated Sardar Bahadur Captain Hira Singh Brar of the Punjab.

"The curse of child marriage is sapping the vitality of thousands of our promising boys and girls on whom the future of our society entirely rests. It is bringing into existence every year thousands of weaklings—both boys and girls—who are born of immature parenthood" (Mahatma Ghandi, *Young India,* 26 August 1926).

Once again, religion demanded that the girl be married before puberty. After that, it was shame. C. V. Krishnaswami Ayyar, social reformer and writer, stated publicly that the Hindu believed marrying daughters after puberty was committing great sin. Caste made it possible, sometimes obligatory, for family members to marry each other.

Mrs. Arunadevi Mukerjei gave evidence from the Baroda Census in 1928: "Out of 28,000 marriages that had been consummated, nearly 22,500 were cases in which the first child is born when the wife was below thirteen years of age."

The *zenana* (harem), an inner room in sometimes the center of eight other outer rooms in a well-to-do home, was nothing less than a prison for a little girl. "Of two places my child will know," said a noble Indian. "This zenana in her home, and when she is twelve she will go in an enclosed litter to her husband's home across the hills, to that zenana."

"Sir, on behalf of the innocent, helpless, suffering girl children of this land, on behalf of millions of child wives, child mothers, and child widows, I appeal to all sections of the House." No one was more vehement than Dr. Mutthulaksmi Reddi in her campaign to end abuses.

Often children were married to old men who died within a few years, leaving the little girl that most despised of all India's creatures—a widow. For a widow is like a snake who devoured her husband's life. Her sins in a past life are being punished by widowhood. "To force widowhood upon little girls is a brutal crime for which we Hindus are daily paying dearly. And does not the Hindu widowhood stink in one's nostrils when one thinks of old and diseased men over fifty taking, or rather purchasing, girl wives, sometimes one on top of another?" asked Mahatma Ghandi, writing in *Young India* (5 August 1926).

The number of widows in British India for the period of 1914-1923 was 26,834,838 according to the Statistical Abstract, an official publication. Close to twenty-seven million widows—most of them children, locked up in houses and huts, disgraced, punished daily, treated as slaves, the object of curses, revilings. Remarriage was forbidden. Child marriages were eventually banned by the British in 1929.

At the time Amy opened a refuge for children in Dohnavur, an Indian widow and high-caste Brahman, Pandita Ramabai Sarasvati, toured the United States pleading for help on behalf of India's children, beseeching Americans — even one — to champion the widows and women of India, but in vain.

Many of Amy's rescued babies were the products of child marriages. Malnutrition began in the womb, and the baby born was undersized and sickly, having a little mother who was often negligent in her mothering, depressed and ill herself. Some of Amy's babies weighed three pounds. The baby's condition was made worse at weaning time when it was placed on watery buttermilk. The little mother had never eaten meat, since the cow was sacred, only cereal grains and the few vegetables the family was able to plant and tend. Only the Untouchables were better nourished; it did not matter what *they* ate!

If the baby survived that far it was in danger of malaria, in a land where 57 million people a year contacted the disease and 1 million died of it. Or, influenza, of which in October and November 1918 7 million persons died.

Jasmine was a child-bride of five years of age and at age twelve a child-widow.

"Your sin from another life ate your husband's life as a vicious snake eats a squirrel!"

"What sin?" wept Jasmine. And because they could not tell her, she cried harder. What had she done?

Her relatives laid hands upon her to shave her head, as was the custom, but her father took pity upon her. "Let her alone until she is sixteen."

For four years Jasmine was a child again and learned to read and write. At age thirteen her jewels were taken from her.

Jasmine's father was a priest whose duty it was to go into the inner shrine and stand before Siva and chant praises and prayers, morning and evening. Little Jasmine went with him and learned all the prayers by heart.

Every morning she performed *puja* (worship), facing east and bathing in water.

"Oh mother river, forgive my sin which killed my husband. Comfort me." At noon and night, the same prayers. "Mine be the refuge of thy lotus feet," she always added, yearning for salvation.

In the evening Jasmine sat by her father in their pleasant little room by a brass lamp, a symbol of the god of fire, Agni. Her father read aloud from his ancient books or recited poetry, and the child's heart longed to know the Supreme God, the Lord over all, He of the lotus feet. Already she loved Him whom she did not know.

Only one thing marred the contentment of those years. Jasmine's mother had born fourteen children, of whom ten died. And of course it was the woman's fault, her sins from a previous life.

Almost every day Jasmine's father dragged his wife into the *ander* behind thick wooden doors and beat her without mercy. The woman had brought only a few dowry jewels to her marriage when she was thirteen, and so his anger flared every time he thought about it. Once she almost died from the beating.

When Jasmine was sixteen the "branding of the widow" took place. Her family embraced her, then threw her down, ripped off her silk sari, and dressed her in coarse white cloth. The village barber shaved her head, as he would do every month for the rest of her life. Now she was the butt of everyone's exasperation and anger and abuse, for had she not caused the death of her innocent husband? Never-ending penance, scraps of leftover garbage for food, crushed with the feeling of always being in the wrong.

Her relatives wept for the poor child, her life blighted by widowhood at age twelve, now at sixteen a widow in every sense of the word.

All of a sudden, during the ceremony, she cried out to them, a sort of prophecy or half-remembered threads of literature from her father's book: "Weep for yourselves, my people! You curse me, but I am blessed! I see a net and threads move as if alive! I see you caught in that net!"

So began a life of tedious seclusion, empty days and years, until she was twenty-seven and her father died. Three years of even more severe penance, fruitless prayers, and obedience to petty rules all in the hope of forgiveness for sin that had slain her husband.

Finally, she was considered old enough to make a pilgrimage, and she traveled all over South India, from one shrine to another, using up her small allowance of money. There were ten thousand people at each festival, so she prayed continually, "God of all, keep me safe." Her shaven head and dress betrayed her, and a widow was fair game for any man.

Words from her father-priest came to mind.

"Seek the Creator, the God of gods." It began to occur to her that the idols of stone and wood were nothing, yet she bowed before them. Still, there was no answer to her prayer to God, the Creator, and she next prayed to die. Rivers and wells and water tanks abounded, and it was not unusual for bodies to be found in them.

"Oh, Thou of the lotus feet, I long for Thee." Of course He had heard, but His plan was to answer her prayer at Dohnavur. So she was led there, worn and sorrowing, and the pilgrimage was over.

"They told me I would find Him here," she said to Amy. "I sought Him in all the temples, but never did I hear a word of Him."

Amy opened the Word of God and revealed to Jasmine Him whom she had ignorantly worshiped. They came to the verse in Psalm 51:16, "Thou desirest not sacrifice, else would I give it," and Jasmine was startled. "The only God I ever met Who said that."

There were days when she almost turned back into unbelief, for cords of love bound her to her large family, and now she was triply accursed in their eyes. There were other voices. "I heard them [the old gods] calling me," she said.

Jasmine was able to read, and mornings she and Amy read together the Old Testament, "the road of the Great Revelation." Afternoons she and Arulai read the New Testament.

One day as Jasmine was reading Isaiah 53, she broke down weeping. "Stop! I cannot bear those words! They stab me as spears!"

That evening her New Testament reading was of the crucifixion.

The realization that God could suffer, and for her, was so powerful that from that day on all her doubts vanished.

"Oh, if only I had heard of Him before! How many years have I lost in not loving Him!"

And to Him she said, "See me at Thy lotus feet, O Lord of my life. Oh, that I had met Thee sooner on the road!"

Forbidden by the British in 1829, *suttee* nevertheless continued, sometimes openly, more often in secret. The little widow, a mere child, sometimes had to be drugged and tied to the funeral pyre. Older girls and women voluntarily threw themselves into the fire, believing in the promise of almost instant paradise for themselves and family.

The whole community longed for and loved a suttee. The moment a widow had so decided, all the neighborhood gathered to be blessed by her.

Amy also knew of the practice of infanticide to get rid of unwanted girl babies, but in her isolated place at Dohnavur was not in direct contact with it. The mere thought of another daughter for whom a dowry must be provided was enough to drive a poor father to leave the baby in a thorn bush where the crows would make short work of it.

A woman who bore only girls was stoned, beaten, or returned in disgrace to her father's house. Sometimes impregnation by a priest was the remedy. The very thought behind the Eastern custom of dowry—that of paying a man to marry a woman—indicated the belief that woman was inferior.

The Sanskrit word for son is *putra,* a "deliverer from hell." Without a son to light the funeral pyre, the father would go for a time to *Put*—hell—

instead of being reincarnated.

Child brides, child widows, the helpless victims of infanticide—all broken jewels, but still jewels.

One of Amy's co-workers, visiting a municipal hospital, spoke of Jesus and His love to a little Brahmin widow. The child was afraid to whisper more than a few words: "After my husband died I was kidnapped—locked up in the temple house—I had to obey—"

"If we could help you, would you like to live with us at Dohnavur?"

The child drew back. The very word *Christian* was a horror to her, signifying all sorts of abominations. But she nodded her consent.

The very brief conversation had been noticed by the child's escort, and she was immediately taken away and sent to another town. All attempts to trace her came to nothing.

Such "failures" to save, humanly speaking, may be classed along with broken jewels. They are unfinished stories, whose end is not in sight.

Fawn, whose father had cursed her, was a jewel in the process of breaking down. Amy was returning from Madras after seeing Walker *Iyer* and his wife off for England. Arulai and Pearleyes (now grown up) were with her, and on the way back they searched for one person whose heart was prepared. "Lord, lead us to souls prepared." They found no one who would even listen to their witness. Was the trip to be in vain? Only this. After dark, an Indian Christian woman met them and told them of Fawn, a child who came to love Jesus and wished to join the Starry Cluster.

Only that. For three months Amy heard no more, until she received a letter from the same Indian woman. "Fawn is so insistent in joining you that I shall send her at once. Her parents have agreed."

Fawn arrived at Dohnavur and happily fit into the life, even winning a younger child to the Lord. Then one day the parents demanded her back, and since Fawn was under age, Amy had no recourse.

"Oh, hide me, hide me!" Fawn cried when she saw her father, but after a minute she controlled herself and faced all the family quietly.

"What does an infant like you know of religion? Are you wiser than your father and his father? Come, enough of this foolishness, come home with us."

"I am a Christian. I cannot live at home."

The father cursed and stormed, the mother wept, the younger sister screamed in a fit of anguish, until Fawn began to waver. Then her father said the wrong thing: "Only come home, and you shall read your Bible and pray, for all gods are one."

Fawn closed her eyes but not in surrender, for she remembered a fire, a Bible thrown in, her two brothers beaten and locked in an inner room. After that, they had changed their minds about being Christians. And she knew the fire would be lighted for her, too.

"Forgive me. I cannot go home."

They departed, but they waited outside the compound wall for darkness to set in. In the Hindu village nearby where no Christian lived, and where the people had never responded to the gospel, the father asked for help in raiding the bungalow and carrying Fawn away by force.

"We will not help you," they all said. "We have no quarrel with the bungalow."

Fawn was saved from her father, but homesickness, depression, longings, and temptations almost too strong to resist set in, and for five years she hovered on the line. After that, prayers and love won, and she grew to be a strong Christian.

Certainly those of any age who set their hands to the plow and draw back can be called broken jewels. So many were merely baptized Hindus, not genuine Christians. Once a man convert took an open stand for Christ, was baptized, and confessed Him to the village. So quickly that all were stunned, first his wife died of cholera, then all three daughters died, then their three husbands, leaving only a grandchild. The heathen around the man continued in good health and prosperity. The man drew back, "lest my little grandson die. He is all I have left."

And the people said, "You have offended a Force whose powers you dared to underestimate. Cease to offend."

In contrast to this sadness, a husband and wife turned to the Lord and burned their items of demon worship. Their four-year-old boy, always strong and well, developed sleeping sickness and paralysis. They brought him to Amy and the other Christians to be prayed for, but he remained unhealed. "Even so, we shall never turn our backs upon God."

"Never mention a need until it has been supplied."

Amy Carmichael

"Then said the giant, 'You practice the craft of a kidnapper gathering up women and children and carrying them into a strange country, to the weakening of my master's kingdom.' "

John Bunyan,
Pilgrim's Progress

8
A Choice Jewel

1902-1938, Dohnavur's growth

In the beginning God created the heavens and earth. While He was working on India He looked down through the ages and saw Amy and the children and knew they would need a secluded spot for safety, far from any well-traveled road. He made almost a desert spot, dry, dusty, with not even any green grass, for it must be unattractive to others. In order that it might blossom as quickly as the violet passion flower, which opens its petals exactly at 9:00 A.M., He created an underground river of sparkling clear water, not exactly under the choice spot, lest flooding be a problem, but close enough so that many streams of water flowing from it were available.

And the Son, without whom was not anything made that was made, saw that it was good. Dohnavur—a choice jewel—but hidden for centuries. He laid a sub-artesian basin so that the well-diggers many years later would rush in great excitement to Amy, saying, "We have struck river sand! Not red earth, but river sand, proving there is a river underground that no one ever knew was in this spot!"

For a family that would use 150,000 gallons of water a day, that was good news! There was no danger of hitting impenetrable rock while well-digging.

At one spot, water spurted out from the barren red rock and scorched sand from only ten feet below the surface, drenching the workers so they were obliged to stop. The inflow of that well proved to be 5,000 gallons an hour.

The Lord God could see ahead to the necessary daily baths, which were a delight to the babies and a rather chilly pleasure to the two-year-olds who sat under the pumps. He could see the fun the Lotus Buds and Teddy Bears would have swimming in an irrigation pond, imitating rotifers they had just seen under a microscope.

And of course He saw Chellalu, that incorrigible child. "Do not go near the well," Amy had warned, "for if you fall in you will drown."

Drown—die—go to heaven—see Jesus. Five-year-old Chellalu smiled widely, all innocence, but her toes wiggled in anticipation.

She had discovered the door to heaven—it was the well! The minute Amy turned her back, going into the supply room to order rice, the minute the coolies left for home, Chellalu began to pile bricks against the well wall, trotting back and forth as fast as her bare feet could manage. She intended to climb up on the slippery rim of the well and go to heaven without further delay.

Dohnavur was a jungle village located in the southwest corner of Tinnevelly District down in the tip of South India, close to the last high rocks of the Ghaut Mountain Range. The barrenness of the place was relieved only by a row of tamarind trees with yellowish wood, covered with pods and red and yellow flowers. The people of the village belonged to the caste called palmyra-climbers.

In 1902, Amy, Ponnammal, the Walkers, the

children, babies, and three nursemaids moved to a spot near Dohnavur where there was a church built in 1824 by money from a German Christian, Count Dohna. The name means "town of Dohna." The family lived in a few broken-down cottages. Walker *Iyer* taught divinity students of the Church Missionary Society, who met at the church. The "choice jewel" was several miles from the road, not too near the village, twenty-four hours from civilization, healthy, and free of malaria.

"God knew what He was doing. He hid you from the eyes of the world for the children's sake," said an Indian Christian lawyer.

Amy still made quick trips into surrounding villages with the Starry Cluster, but more and more she was tied to the babies and children who saw no good reason for her leaving them for a single moment.

Invitations came to speak and teach at conventions from the Reformed Syrian Church in Travancore, but Amy refused. Calls to address large groups came from other parts of India. Her reply to all was no. She grieved over the many people, willing to sit and listen to God's Word, without a teacher, but was comforted remembering that Jesus once washed feet. He "took a towel" (John 13:4) and by that raised work to a high and dignified level anywhere but especially in a land where such work of child-caring was left to the lowest. There were no English "nannies," and Amy would not allow unbelievers to raise the children.

"Demeaning work," a Christian pastor said, discouraging the only woman at the time who thought of volunteering.

But Amy knew if she reared Indian children to

be strong Christians, they could do more for Him among their own people than a foreigner ever could. She would be multiplying herself over and over in the lives of the children, helping India evangelize India.

In 1903, the Walkers returned to England, since Mrs. Walker was very ill. The little handful at Dohnavur were left completely unprotected, humanly speaking, with only a low mud wall around the compound. There was no man with them to even deter evildoers.

The arrival of the second infant, Sapphire, made Amy do some serious thinking and praying. She had prayed for more and more babies to be prevented from entering the temple stronghold of Satan. More babies meant more nurseries. Bricks would be needed. How to begin?

The Imp and Tangles and eleven-year-old Lotus and eight-year-old Mouse all slept comfortably next to Amy in one of the cottages, but babies needed their own special place.

Amy went for a walk and prayed as she walked, adding sums in her head, figuring the cost of bricks. When she returned, she found the mail had arrived, and in it was a check for the very amount she had decided upon. And, a third baby was rescued.

She purchased a small piece of land, a field, right there and immediately received an anonymous gift of two hundred rupees earmarked "for the nursery." Who knew of the need? She had told no one.

In India a small plot of land may be owned by dozens, even scores, of people through a system of inheritance called "fragmentation." When a man died his land was divided among his sons, perhaps six sons. When the six died, their land was chopped up again among male heirs. If the six sons each had four sons, the original small plot of perhaps one-half acre was then twenty-four slivers. One person might own 1/6 of the northern quarter of a sliver. Each reluctant paternal uncle's cousin's third wife's sister's son had to be found and friendship established, before any negotiations could be made.

Sometimes fractions of slivers of land were owned jointly by several people, one of them refusing to sell, and with no visible boundary lines to be seen. The total land in Dohnavur was purchased in 171 pieces ranging from 1/100 of an acre to 7 and 38/100 of an acre. Patience! A most valuable virtue in the East.

The year passed quickly, and Walker *Iyer* returned from England with Amy's mother. Mrs. Walker stayed behind, too unwell to travel. Mrs. Carmichael was delighted to be part of a family of thirty people, from the youngest nine-month-old baby to their thirty-four-year-old "Amma"—Amy. Mrs. Carmichael loved them all in the special way a grandma loves.

Everyone slept on grass mats, with a cotton sheet on top if the weather was cool. Days, the mats and sheets were rolled up and stacked out of the way. All the children helped scrub the red floor tiles until they shone, especially since the dining table was just a banana leaf laid on a mat on the floor. Most meals were rice eaten with curries, chutney, or pickles. The children learned to dip only the fingers of the right hand into the rice, and no deeper than the first knuckles of the fingers.

"Hate not laborious work. Joy, joy is in it." The children sang one of Amy's made-up choruses as they swept paths clear of garbage and carried buckets of water from well and pump to keep flowers and plants alive.

Then, out of the clear blue Indian sky, measles struck down seven children, and being Indian they took it ten times harder than their English cousins.

No doctor, no registered nurse, no foster mother. "It is not our custom," the village women said to Amy after she made a desperate trip into town with a dying baby in her arms, hoping for a wet nurse.

The beloved Amethyst came down with dysentery, weakened, died. Amy's mother, who had raised seven healthy children, tried everything, studied the few medical books they owned, but had no idea what to do. No one did. Indian children seemed to come into the world weak and tending to illness.

In studying the Bible together, in reading the lives of saints and pioneers, Amy and Ponnammal both saw a pattern laid out that God gave to His servants in all ages, a little at a time. At the center of the pattern like the hub of a wheel, was this: Seek God's will before asking anything. Then ask, and it will surely be given. Sometimes the prayer must be, "Thy will be done—whatever it is."

Whoever said, "Make haste slowly," described the way the Dohnavur Fellowship was built.

Not, "Hear, Lord, for Thy servant speaketh," but, "Speak, Lord, for Thy servant is listening." Amy learned more and more to listen. The work she was called to do was too time-consuming and expensive to make mistakes. There was only one possible exception in regard to waiting, but even that was based on the knowledge of God's will. Whenever they heard of a baby or child in danger, not a moment was wasted. One of them left immediately to the rescue.

The giving or withholding of financial help was taken, as it has been from time immemorial, as an indication of the Father's approval. No one was on salary. Neither did they ever go into debt.

She often read from the life of George Mueller of Bristol, England, where he said something like this: People say that I am unique in trusting God alone to supply the daily bread for the thousands of orphans. They say only George Mueller has this special gift of faith. True, the work was begun to take in these homeless children, but that was not the number one purpose. I wanted to show the world that God is alive and will answer prayers of faith, and the orphanages are to be a living memorial to that fact.

And love, shining love, that set no limits, bound all the family together.

The London Missionary Society at Neyyoor, one and one-half day's journey away by bandy, was a medical mission. They agreed to help Amy open a nursery there, where the weaker babies might stay close to doctors and nurses. In September 1905, Ponnammal braved a hurricane and took some of the ill babies to Neyyoor Nursery. Eight months later, she was in charge of fifteen babies in four small houses with the help of three nursing women and five young Christian girls in nurses' training.

The next year cholera swept through the area surrounding Dohnavur in a raging epidemic, but never entered the compound of the family. Amy visited the village people, having nothing but permanganate of potash to give plus her own cheerful encouragement.

After six new converts were baptized, Satan retaliated by attacking the babies at Neyyoor. Sixteen came down with dysentery, and ten died. Each one of the ten had been redeemed at great personal cost to someone. But they had cost Jesus most, said Amy. "He is only an owner in name who has no right to do as he will with his own."

Amy herself was so worn out that the doctor ordered her to the cooler heights of Ootacamund for a rest, and she took twelve of the children with her. Oh, for another Ponnammal! The need for helpers with medical training was imperative.

Overcrowding in the nursery at Dohnavur promoted the spread of any infection, so Amy rejoiced when money came earmarked for "new nurseries." Ponnammal was then able to return, bringing the babies. She had been gone two and one-half years.

Chellalu kept dropping in to liven things up.

"Chellalu, come down," Amy had called softly, so as not to startle her. That incorrigible one reluctantly turned her back on the door of heaven and did not jump into the well. She devoted her time, instead, to language usage, for she had learned some English words.

A foreign lady was visiting and spied Chellalu, sitting in the middle of the path, hoping to be noticed. "What is your name, little girl?"

"Yesh-no."

"Are you happy here, sweetheart?"

"Yesh-no."

"And what did you have for dinner, dear?"

"Yesh-no."

Dates are dull, but necessary. Dates are as impersonal as pages of a calendar turning over, but they serve to give a quick overall picture of how the Dohnavur Fellowship grew.

In 1907, the first registered nurse, Mable Wade, arrived at Dohnavur, the first European to join the Fellowship. At nicely spaced intervals God also sent three trained teachers.

In 1909, *Lotus Buds,* the book of photos and vignettes of nursery life, was published. Three years after, when the civilized and Christian world began to hear of temple children, Queen Mary wrote Amy a note of sympathy and encouragement.

During one of those days, a note and small gift of money arrived from a little girl in England: "I wanted so much to buy a doll and name it Chellalu, but after I prayed I decided to send you the money instead to save another baby."

There was one Sunday morning when all who loved Chellalu feared she may have been destined for a stage career. As the family sat in church and Walker *Iyer* preached, enlivening the sermon with magnificent gestures, Chellalu slipped away from her mat and somehow managed to get behind him. She mimicked him perfectly. She waved an arm, clenched a fist, stalked foward, stepped back, keeping right behind the *Iyer's* long legs.

Amy and all watched in horrified silence, but Chellalu tactfully ended her performance after a few minutes and dropped down upon her mat.

By 1917, the Dohnavur family numbered 140. The weather, as usual, was hot—hotter—hottest! The hill resorts for Europeans could be reached only by long, expensive railroad trips. Nine miles from Dohnavur, high in the green mountains, 3,000 feet above sea level, lay an abandoned coffee garden of forty acres with a pool of pure water on the property. The Muslim owner asked for 100 pounds, an out-of-sight price for Amy. She prayed, and God sent three separate gifts of 100 pounds each, confirming her desire three times over. She bought the land and remembered her own earlier words, "The secret of going on is to get away."

She and the children climbed up the mountainside and camped there to supervise the building of Forest House for much-needed vacations. There was a shrine to the "Demon of the Chain" on the site, and after Amy and the children knocked it down, the laborers alternated between fear, complaining, mutiny, and squabbling over caste. Of work they did little until, shamed by the way the little ones pitched in to help, carrying loads of sand and stone up a steep slope from the river bed, they grudgingly put in a little time. Twice the walls they built fell almost on top of them.

Each night Amy held a meeting, and two of the men were converted to Christ. All who had threatened to quit, stayed. For, Amy explained, if they were to go the angels would surely come down and help.

Forest House was surrounded by mountains on three sides. To the east, the jungle dropped down to red plains and the distant blue sea. A river cascaded through a rocky ravine. The deep pool was christened the "Emerald Pool," perfect for diving and swimming. Wild pineapples and oranges grew in profusion.

The place was blessed with birds and bugs and

flowers of rare species. Elephants, tigers, panthers, bears, deer, wild dogs, monkeys, and mountain goats promised excitement.

Forest House spelled a blessed relief from the worst of the heat, a place where a tired *sittie* or *accal* might sleep all day if she chose.

Amy discovered that baby boys also were in moral danger in the temples, and in 1918 the first baby boy was rescued. The year 1923 saw thirty nurseries filled with fat, jolly babies and growing children. In 1924, Dr. May Powell joined the Fellowship. In 1925, the family amicably ceased to be affiliated with the Church of England Zenana Missionary Society and was legally organized the following year as the Dohnavur Fellowship.

Dr. Godfrey Webb-Peploe came to work with the little boys, and his brother, Murray, followed.

Another interruption from Chellalu. She had been very naughty, and her *sittie* wrote all the crimes down on a note and sent her to Amy. What would "Amma" say, and—worse—what might she do? Chellalu dared not throw the note away. She dared not avoid Amma. All at once she saw the solution.

"Amma, it is Chellalu." She waited on Amy's doorstep.

"Why aren't you in school?"

"*Sittie* sent me with a note."

Amy looked stern. "Where *is* the note?"

Chellalu beamed at her charmingly. "Amma, I've eaten it!"

By 1929, the family of 700 began to build a hospital called *Parama Suha Saloi*—Place of Heavenly Healing. Though Amy could no longer visit the villages, the villagers now came to her. She had first prayed about a hospital in 1921. Fifteen years later it was completed.

A gift of 1,000 pounds was prayed for as a sign from the Lord. On Amy's birthday in 1929 a cable reported the gift was on its way. Soon after, another 1,000 pounds was given. The rest of the 10,000 pounds needed for a hospital was made up of small amounts, some of it pennies from children around the world who heard of Dohnavur. By 1938, the Dohnavur Fellowship was spread over 170 acres.

"The teacher who is attempting to teach without inspiring the pupil with a desire to learn is hammering on cold iron."

Horace Mann

"Children should not be exposed to more than one way to cross a *t*."

Amy Carmichael

9
Polishing the Jewels

1902-1929, The Father's children

The brilliant, flashing chatoyancy in a rough tigereye gemstone is released by a number of violent and painful methods.

First, the stone is blasted out of its solid rock vein or stabbed with pick and hammer. The stone is then thrown onto a conveyer belt and taken above ground. In a gemcutter's workshop, the stone is gripped in a vise, cut with a saw, ground with a coarse wheel, sanded, polished with tin oxide, and pierced with a drill.

Or, in the case of tumbled stones, the tigereye is locked into a rock-polishing machine for four weeks, no privacy, tossed about with all sorts of companions, scratched, irritated by rough grit almost the hardness of a diamond. Either process is a most unpleasant experience for the tigereye.

The finished product is a radiant jewel of deep honey color, flashing bands of silky gold light, fit for a maharaja's crown.

"Nothing was ever made easy for her. She was too precious to spoil by the easy." Amy's way of preparing the child Arulai for life and service carried over to all her children. Nothing was made easy for them in body, mind, or spirit. Amy demanded absolute truthfulness. "Truth in the inner being" (Psalm 51:6, *The Amplified Bible*). This love of truthfulness was the foundation for courage and all right living.

One of the little tots who owned a rag doll coveted a piece of lace to go around its shoulders, sari-style. She saw the lace on someone else's prettier doll, ripped it off when no one was looking, and tied it around *her* rag doll.

The sermon that Sunday was on the sin of Achan, who stole a Babylonian garment, then hid it. Baby though she was, her conscience bit her. She tore the lace from her doll and buried it in the garden where no one would ever find it.

That night she couldn't sleep. She felt just too Achan-like, and the Word of God burned even in the soul of a three-year-old. When Amy answered her crying, the story came out. They went, hand in hand, with a lantern and dug up the bit of lace. They prayed together. The sin was forgiven, and the lesson of truthfulness was stamped on the child's mind forever.

Amy always made sure the punishment fit the crime. A child who had wantonly stripped a flower of its petals was asked to fit them back on. A quarrelsome, antisocial child was put into a small barrel reaching her shoulders until she grew bored with her own company and wished to make friends again.

Hard work was part of life at Dohnavur. He who would help souls must demand something of them. From nursery days on, Amy demanded much of her children. Their reward was not money or treats but to be trusted with harder work.

One young convert loved to sit on the floor reading her Bible or gazing dreamily off at the mountain view outside the window, waiting for the dinner bell. She soon learned that to be happy she must contribute her share to the happiness of the rest of the family. After Amy's loving explanation and example (for she worked right along with the children), the girl gladly took her turn at scrubbing pots and pans.

Even the five-year-olds helped carry away over fifteen tons of broken masonry after the men and older boys had destroyed an idol shrine on a newly purchased piece of property. Children with baskets of mud balanced on their heads also helped clear away a wall that the monsoon rains brought crashing down in millions of pieces.

Paths must be swept, bedding aired, gardens watered by hand, pots scoured using a handful of grass and some ashes, floor tiles polished until they gleamed and reflected.

Amy understood children needed stories on their own level, but she avoided English fairy tales. They were just too foreign for the Indian child. "Please do not tell my little girl any fairy tales," said a village gentleman. "The spirits are real to us — and they are all bad."

"*Me' thān ā?*" Is it really true?

"*Me' thān ā.*" True indeed.

How much better that response to stories, she thought. So she wrote her own stories for the children. Books, mountains, forests, sea, and music Amy listed as the chief instructors in her school. She had the advantage in that the children were sheltered from all other influences.

She taught by action songs where the children learned the words in English and acted out the habits of birds and animals. A microscope opened up that new world for them. They studied both

113

English and Tamil, reciting lessons in a sing-song chant.

Amy's goal was to train good soldiers for Jesus Christ, academic accomplishments being secondary.

If love, truth, and hard work were the foundations of Dohnavur, music built the walls. Amy found the words of many English hymns ambiguous, archaic, even ridiculous—certainly not understandable to an Indian child.

Once she inquired about a little dying boy who had been with them only a short time. "What is he doing?"

"He is lying on his mat, making tunes."

Two days later he was still singing but with the great angelic choirs.

"There was something in that place that could only be seen through prayerful eyes," wrote a clergyman who visited Dohnavur. "The three hundred children lived in cottages, each cottage under an Indian girl with about a dozen tiny ones in her charge.

"How much do you pay these young women to care for all these children?" he asked.

"The lady [Amy] replied, 'It is very expensive work, for they have to be up at all hours of the day and night—it is too expensive to pay for, so none of us gets any salary; we all do it through love.'

"And love in turn brought forth joy. I have never seen such joy on the faces of people. They shine!"

"What will you do with them later?" asked another sort of visitor, eying the mats of babies, the clusters of happily active little tots.

"You will live to regret it!" was the stern pronouncement of another.

Amy could not help wondering about the children's future if they were not educated. She would not accept less than dedicated Christians who desired to build in gold, silver, and precious stones. Other missionaries in India agreed with her that mission schools were not turning out Christians with strong character and a firm faith that nothing could shake.

She saw the need for both women and men who would give up married life and "attend upon the Lord without distraction," as Arulai said. She and Pearleyes, now grown up, had made that decision, and their lives were spent in the Dohnavur Fellowship work.

Amy felt that if ever unloving attitudes were allowed to creep into the Fellowship, there would be spiritual decay. Do such standards seem visionary? Amy held to them and so attracted workers of high quality.

Sisters of the Common Life was formed by seven Christian girls at Dohnavur who decided God's will for them did not include marriage. Others were added to the group through the years, and Amy came to count on them, to ask anything from them, knowing they would refuse nothing for the Lord. Amy's advice to them was the same she would have given any missionary: Guard against depression. Bear evenly with all that is uneven. Never be shocked out of loving.

Sister Paula alone traveled a total of 25,000 miles to save fifty-nine children.

A corn of wheat falls into the ground and dies alone, in darkness, allowing itself to be changed, cut off from sun and air. But, oh, the harvest! A hundredfold!

"Each child felt itself the only child in the family, so lovingly was each cherished and so abundant was the thanksgiving over virtuous behavior," Amy said.

The children tended to avoid what was difficult, but once the will was seized and trained in the right direction it held as firm as a steel rod. An Indian child loved with all his mind and strength.

"Even if they are saved from temple life," wrote an Indian reviewer of one of Amy's books, "of what use will they ever be? They will revert to type."

"Perhaps you are on the wrong track," remarked an acquaintance after a baby died of poisoned milk. "The work seems so difficult and wasteful."

Amy learned to shrug off such comments, though they buzzed around her head like stinging insects. The children were worth any personal suffering.

Those teaching the children often survived temperatures of 100-110° in the shade. *"His leaf shall not wither" was written for Europeans in India*, Amy thought humorously.

One day in the kindergarten, Chellalu decided against listening, brought out a long piece of red tape from her pocket, tied her feet together, curled up on the bench, and seemed to be asleep. The teacher did not disturb her. She may have been grateful!

Question time came, and the children, smitten by the grave story of Abraham offering his only son, gave very serious answers. One baby brushed away a few tears.

"What did Isaac say to his father as they walked up the mountain together?"

Chellalu suddenly uncurled, sat up, and replied: "He said, 'Father, do not kill me!' Yesh! That was what he said."

Arulai, grown up and a teacher, believed that the impressions made upon the mind of a little child would last forever. Once the Bible story for the day was the Good Samaritan. The little tots were scandalized at the behavior of the priest and Levite. "Punish them! Give them whippings!" they urged. One little tot left her seat and solemnly marched up to the picture of the departing priest and Levite. "Take care what you are doing!" she said in Tamil, shaking one fat brown finger at them. Then in English, "Naughty! Naughty!"

The Dohnavur children were a delight, but ever uppermost in Amy's thoughts were the others.

She was harrassed by court cases, legal battles that sometimes dragged on for years. To be the object and subject of criminal cases, one after another! To be the center of such publicity, when publicity was dreaded!

Legally, Amy's hands were shackled. In 1912 she heard of a young girl who escaped from her life of degradation and fled to a missionary asking for protection. He could not give it, and the girl was forced back into her home. In despair she drowned herself.

The law punished only the offense, not the intent to commit, or even the preparation, unless it amounted to an attempt under the Penal Code. She sent carefully prepared case histories of temple women who "adopted" children, the adoption being merely the "taking" of a child. It was impossible to prove there was no legal adoption since papers could be forged, false witnesses produced. Even if there was proof that a child was not legally adopted by a temple woman, the court would only return the child to her own home, which could be a place little better than the temple.

One sure indication that a child was destined for temple life was instruction in dancing. No good Hindu parents allowed their children to dance. Even the Untouchable women did not dance, with the exception of devil dancers, mostly old women.

An Indian lawyer Amy knew deplored the fact that the government was helpless to pass laws to save children from the temples. The letter of the law must be respected—that the British government would not interfere in matters of religion. The Indian lawyer was saddened whenever he thought of it.

Any attempt to encourage a child to come to Amy or any assistance given to help her to escape would render her liable to prosecution for kidnapping—a criminal offense under law.

Amy's Indian sisters stood in dread of the very word *prison,* for *himsa*—torture to obtain confession—was common. The *accals* were all young Christians, shy as Indian women were, yet over and over they faced the possibility that Amy could be arrested, convicted of kidnapping, and sentenced to seven years in an Indian prison. They could easily imagine what would happen to a family of women and children left completely without protection.

They not only faced it bravely, in faith, but each one of them said, "Let me be *buthil*—the substitute. Let me go to prison in your place!"

Did Amy ever regret getting involved in such a risky work? Never. Even if there were no other rewards, the children rewarded them.

Four-year-old Pyarie and Tingalu, side by side, walked demurely to kindergarten class. They carried toys in both hands but dutifully laid them on a table until story time would be over. Arulai was telling of the Unmerciful Servant. To help them understand on their level, she explained that the baby who snatched all the toys was unfair and selfish. Such a baby might even grow up to be like the Unmerciful Servant!

Pyarie and Tingalu looked at the picture, and then at each other. "Oh, bad, nasty man!" they chimed together. "Very, very bad," Pyarie made it understood.

Prayer over, they both rushed to the table to get their toys. Pyarie reached them first and swept them all into her arms, turning to run. A word from Arulai stopped her. There was a struggle inside the baby heart. Then she ran to Tingalu and thrust all the toys into her lap. Jumping into Arulai's arms she cried, "*Accal!* Am I not a *merciful* servant?"

"Did Peter and John talk English or Tamil?" a confused little girl whispered to her neighbor after hearing the story of the lame man and the disciples.

"Tamil, of course," said the second child, no doubt at all in her mind.

An older girl, able to express herself more eloquently, once said after being scolded for disobedience: "Within my heart wrath burned like a fire, but my mouth could not open to reply, for inside me a voice said, 'It is true, entirely true. Accal is perfectly just.' "

Sellamutthu was that *accal*. She once traveled the equivalent distance from London to Moscow and back to save little Suseela.

The children's worship service on Sunday was only a half hour long, begun with a moment of silence, with another space of silence halfway through. The service was a joy, and the children looked forward to it all week. Thank offerings were given, something of the children's own, usually a sticky sweet (sucked only a little while), and once a teddy bear, which was returned (like Isaac off the altar) to the relieved child.

Amy once took a group of older children for an educational tour of Madras, and they visited a jeweler to see the uncut stones. The children easily identified and described each gem. "Where did they learn anything about this?" the surprised man asked. "From reading the book of Revelation," Amy replied.

Tuesday and Friday evenings were given to demon worship throughout India. Drums, animal noise, cries of dancers continued all night long and could be heard from nearby villages. The older children and the new converts remembered the old life. Nightmares, spiritual strain, sometimes defeat marked those nights. True, most of the demon worship was hundreds of miles away, but miles did not matter when spirit forces pulled.

Every bedtime was preceded with prayer and singing, but those two nights, especially, were fortified with extra time with the children, private prayer with any who were fearful, ending with the beautiful chorus "Jesus, Tender Shepherd, Hear Us."

The old hymn assures us that "hell's foundations quiver," but Amy often said a missionary's own foundations quivered under satanic attack.

Amy lived a double life all those years. One life was as a happy, laughing companion and mother to the children. The other life was hidden, a living grief over the millions of children who had no help. Not that the innocent suffered, but that the innocent sinned, is what discouraged them.

Lakshmi was such a child, but her story ended happily. She was a seven-year-old slave of the gods. She and Tara listened one night after the old priest had called for little Esli. They heard her screams. "They cannot make me do it," Tara whispered. "I will save myself."

The next morning her body was found in the well.

Lakshmi had attended a mission school long enough to memorize the following: "Lighten-our-darkness-we-beseech-thee-O-Lord-and-by-thy-great-mercy-defend-us-from-all-perils-and-dangers-of-this-night-for-the-love-of-Thine-only-Son-our-Savior-Jesus-Christ."

She repeated it to an Indian lady doctor she visited, who explained it to her in Tamil. *My mantra*, Lakshmi thought.

The night she made her first appearance on a stage in the temple with men worshipers packed around her so close they could touch her, she was frightened, and the prayer flashed through her mind. There was a burst of torchlight, a blast of music, and before she realized what she was doing she dropped to her knees and repeated her "mantra."

The temple woman beside her pinched her arm painfully and forced her to her feet, and she danced. Seven years old, married to the gods — and to their worshipers.

One night, covering her bright clothes with a long servant's scarf, she slipped out of the house and ran down the street, anywhere. A man tore away her scarf and shouted, "A slave of the gods, running away!"

Lakshmi, terrified, began to chant her "mantra" aloud as she ran. She turned down a narrow street, and a white woman stepped out from a doorway. With a cry for help, Lakshmi sprang into her arms, gasping ". . . for-the-love-of-our-Savior-Jesus-Christ!" and fainted.

"What does this mean?" the lady asked.

"It is a devadasi. She belongs to our god. Give her to us." The mob threatened to attack, but the white woman shielded the child. "She has claimed my help in the name of Jesus Christ, *my* Lord," she said. "Fall back!" They circled around, still muttering, but finally left, and she carried the child to safety.

"My mantra, my charm, worked," said Lakshmi afterward. "What can I do for your Lord who saved me? Can I dance for Him and sing?"

The white woman, a missionary, explained that the words Lakshmi learned to parrot were not a mantra, but prayer to a living God, which He had answered. Lakshmi came to love Him, but for a year after that someone had to sleep and eat and live every moment with her to clear her mind of the loathsome things she had been taught in speech and deed and thought.

About this time the little Soldanella found her way to Dohnavur. A lawsuit was brought against her and the two friends that helped her, and Amy represented the child in court. More than 2,400 miles of travel were made on Soldanella's behalf. Finally the case ended. "Dismissed." The courthouse was burned down by an angry mob, but Soldanella was safe.

Polish — to give perfecting touches. The children were polished by love, truthfulness, hard work, discipline; reinforced by Scripture, prayer, and song. And while she was polishing, in each day that went from 5:00 A.M. to 10:00 P.M., Amy herself was being strengthened for even more difficult times.

"If everyone who reads this letter will sit down right now and write out a check for $25 — $50 — $100 — we might be able to pay our bills and not go under. We are deeply in debt, and only you . . ."

Newsletter today

"Your Heavenly Father knoweth that ye have need of all these things."

Matthew 6:32

10
Jewels of the Ledger

1900-1935, The Father's provision

"Why not just pray for a thousand pounds?" asked a Lotus Bud, watching Amy carefully recording sums in a ledger book. "That would make everything so nice and easy."

"Nice and easy," Amy explained, "would turn our faith to jelly." Then she was obliged to explain "jelly" to the Indian child.

Prayer was a part of Amy's life since her very first prayer at age three, to which the answer was no. This chapter deals with Amy's answers to prayer from the beginning of her work with children, centered mainly on the ledger that reported needs, requests to the Father, and answers in black and white.

In 1904, a letter came from a pastor friend who lived a six-hour journey by train from Dohnavur telling of a child about to be dedicated to Siva. "They have spent 100 rupees on the festivities. Can you send the money at once to repay them? They will give you the child." (Fifteen rupees then equalled one pound sterling.)

Amy had less than an hour to decide. How could she refuse? Ponnammal left with the money and returned safely with the little girl, but Amy and Ponnammal were both disturbed over paying money directly to the devil. Amy prayed for a sign of God's approval, a round sum of 100 rupees to replace the money sent. It arrived. "I was writing out a check for a different sum but Someone changed my mind," read the note with it.

After that, every journey to save a child was expensive in time, money, and energy, but "special sums dropped as if from the skies to meet these unexpected charges."

Babies demanded nurseries. Amy was given enough money to build a room 24 by 12 feet. "Why not add on a porch for shade and play space when rain prevents outdoor exercise?" someone asked. The Indian builders too, were puzzled over the lack of a proper veranda.

That it was very sensible Amy agreed, and replied that their heavenly Father would give that if they asked Him. She stopped the building of the nursery for four days so they could pray about it. Two days later (not even on their usual mail day), a letter arrived with 200 rupees labeled, "For a new nursery." Then another 100 rupees. Then fifty. The Hindu masons were impressed. Truly, Amy's God was alive and listening and very kind.

Once Amy was in the crowded railroad station at Tinnevelly Bridge praying for a need she had not even mentioned to Ponnammal or Sellamutthu, her closest companions. An unknown hand tucked an envelope of money into *her* hand just as she hurriedly boarded the train. "God's ravens," she called such friends, flying about where ravens are not usually found.

Amy kept a cash box with small amounts of money in it to be used only for quick trips to save babies and children.

Dohnavur was four hundred miles away from their bank in which funds for the work were kept.

And a check could be obtained only by going to the mission office at Palamcottah, a day's journey away. A rash of robberies on the roads between had discouraged any communication. One day a telegram arrived by usual government mail: "Send money order by return mail to save this child 800 miles away." Impossible? Along with the telegram was a money order gift from Canada for the exact sum of money needed. All Amy had to do was sign it, slip it into an envelope, and hand it to the waiting postman. The child was saved.

"I thought Indian babies lived on rice water!" was one woman's remark after hearing forty pounds had been spent on milk.

When Ponnammal was at the Neyyoor Nursery with the sick babies, skimping and doing without for herself as much as possible, always economical, it was necessary to pay a bill of 100 rupees. Amy didn't have the money, but she prayed. The next week a money order arrived for 151 rupees.

One day Amy stood on the porch of a new nursery and gazed across a long field reaching clear up to the outskirts of a village on the north.

"Ask for that piece of land," came the inner voice she had learned to recognize.

"Lord, I don't *want* that piece of land!"

"Ask anyhow."

Such an experience had never been hers, to ask for something she didn't want. Obediently she asked, adding candidly, "But have we not enough?"

Gifts of money began to come for the field, one all the way from Africa. A large gift arrived from one who wrote, "I am sure the Lord wants you to expand."

In later years, Amy could look back and see the reason for buying the unwanted field. Without actually encroaching on the land, villagers were moving closer and closer to Dohnavur, sinking wells and staying permanantly. "We feel safe, living near you," they said. However, they also would have bought up bits of the field, slice by slice, until Dohnavur would have been smothered and unsafely close to too many people. Now, the north was bounded by fields of rice and grain.

Babies were bound to grow up into children. Children meant schooling. Amy asked God to show her a pattern for a schoolhouse, if it was His will. Again, the pattern shown was "too big, too large. And why so costly?" Amy had received a sum of money to cover a smaller building. The estimate of the larger building given on January 17, 1910, far exceeded the money on hand.

Amy, already embroiled in another court case to save a child, studied the sketch of the proposed large schoolhouse, perplexed. Would they ever have children to fill *that* space?

On the twenty-ninth of the month, 36 pounds arrived by mail, enough for the foundation of the new building. "We will build only as money is supplied," Amy told the masons.

In February, a delayed letter arrived, dated January 17, the day Amy had prayed about the pattern for building. "One hundred pounds is on its way" was the happy message. Amy ran out into the field and showed the letter to the masons. After that, there was a steady surprise of gifts, over and above usual needs, earmarked "for building."

When finished, the school building was large enough to seat all the family whenever they celebrated festivities and held Sunday worship. Because birthdays of the children were mostly unknown, the "Coming Day" of each one's arrival at Dohnavur was celebrated. Written on the wall of the schoolhouse was a verse that had for the family a double meaning, "I will bless the Lord Who has given me counsel," chosen by the child Amy won in the court battle.

Things did not always operate smoothly and routinely in a "prayer-answer, prayer-answer" way. One month, when funds on hand amounted to 15 pounds instead of the average 66, a letter arrived from an Indian who claimed that a fraction of one of the land slices was his, sold while he was out of town. He was prepared to take the matter to court. Amy had barely recovered from two years of court trouble (and its expenses), and a nursery was already half-built upon that gentleman's "slice."

What was there to do? Amy prayed.

And that was the end of the matter. No more letters came, and the gentleman never made an appearance. God made up for the lean month, and that year ended with an excess of 262 pounds.

On December 23, 1913, Amy prayed for guidance and a sign if she was to purchase another slice of land whose owners asked 450 rupees as a down payment. Land was added, little by little. The very next day, the Christmas Eve mail produced 500 rupees from an unknown giver. "Great cheer!" Amy wrote in her diary, describing both the birthday festivities of the Lord and the answered prayer. For ten and one half years she continued buying up slices of land.

"We ask . . . He heareth . . . we have" (1 John 5:14-15). But it must always be "according to His will." Amy put prayer matters in their right order. First, seek God's will, many times plainly given in His Word, such as, He is "not willing that any should perish" (2 Peter 3:9). If Amy was not led to a verse of Scripture, the next step was to continue to pray and ask God to reveal His will. Once known, His will may be prayed for, confident of the answer. Not, "Bless my plans and bring them to pass," nor, "Change Thy will and conform it to mine."

World War 1 spelled shock to the Dohnavur Fellowship and confusion to the villagers, who predicted ruin and collapse for Dohnavur.

"Is it safe to trust only God?" they asked. "In a war the mails will be lost." They watched, waited, tongues smacking over dire and awful predictions, but the day came when they said in awe, "Their God feeds them!"

The Dohnavur Fellowship grew until they owned rice fields, a farm, herds of cattle, gardens. One year after the seedbeds were planted near the end of October, weather unexpectedly turned hot and dry. Thousands of caterpillars, hearing the sun's call, woke up and hatched out of their cocoons, spied the seedlings, and began to feast. Amy and all the family right down to five-year-olds began to pray, since it seemed the whole crop would be lost. They prayed also for the village people and their crops.

Two days later, they all went out to look at the field. Hundreds of white egrets were busy devouring the caterpillars, and by next day no caterpillars were left, and the rice crop was saved.

This time God protected only the crops of the Dohnavur Fellowship, who openly called Him

Lord, and the crops of the villagers who prayed to idols for help were destroyed.

During a trying time when Ponnammal lay dying of cancer, Amy asked God to send money in cash to tide them over. She prayed that prayer at 5:30 A.M. The 8:00 A.M. mail delivered a large registered envelope containing 3,000 rupees—all in small notes. "Before they call . . !"

In September 1917, all of Amy's workers agreed with her about rescuing baby boys, the only hesitation caused by the lack of medical help. (Amy prayed for a doctor for fourteen years.) On the eighth of the month a medical student offered to come to Dohnavur and was welcomed with open arms. The first baby boy arrived January 14, 1918. Amy had discovered they, too, were in moral danger, being given to the temples and trained as musicians. Another nursery was needed. The Lord seemed to draw her and say, "Ask," and she asked for 100 pounds *to arrive the next day*.

The mail was duly delivered by the postman who up-ended his sack and scattered letters to the four winds, in his usual way. Forty-two rupees, six annas, three more rupees. "Has the 100 pounds been given?" the family all asked, from the little ones on up. "No, but it will come," said Amy. No letters remained to be opened.

Even as she spoke, a worker entered the room and put a check into her hands, a legacy she had just received. It was 100 pounds.

Only once, during 1919, they hit rock bottom financially with only 35 pounds to their name. Life seemed like a pair of forceps with rapidly closing points, and the space between them was not comfortable!

"Will money seen in a dream pay bills? Will rice eaten in a dream satisfy hunger?" the Tamil proverb taunted her, but prayer, the vital breath of the soul, buoyed her up. Is it not easier to breathe than to hold one's breath? That breath gives life to the whole body. Without breath (prayer) the body is dead. Prayer was Amy's very breath as she paced the courtyard one fear-filled night during the war and pictured the children starving to death and the Christian world blaming her.

The gifts were not always money. In England the Dohnavur Fellowship secretary was given a beautiful shawl by a blind woman who was dying. When sold it realized two pounds for Dohnavur. A poor girl gave a workbasket and two cups and saucers. An elderly man gave the gold piece he had saved for his old age.

In Ireland, an eight-year-old boy, reading of the Dohnavur children, saved his pennies and bought a few toys at a time until he could pack a box full. The box was sent on the ship *Roumania*, which was lost in the Bay of Biscay. Eight-year-old Robin thought of all the pretty toys now at the bottom of the sea, the children who might not have toys for Christmas, and he was unhappy. His mother offered to advance him money she meant to spend on his own Christmas present to replace the toys. He thought it over for a few hours, then ran to her, his face aglow. "Mother, I want to do it! Let's hurry and go shopping again!"

An older boy in another part of the world sent his first week's wages. And a crumpled wad of paper with a shilling inside arrived at Dohnavur, the note reading, "Fur Miss Karmikal from won wot carnt afford more."

Some of the gifts, Amy firmly believed, were divinely chosen no matter what their reaction to them. For example, who in the world would send a sharp razor to a nursery? Yet a razor arrived in a package one day just when an older boy was complaining that a barber of his particular caste simply must be found—an impossibility—or he would not, could not, shave, could not work, attend classes or church, or appear in public. Behold—a razor—just in time for the long journey he must take. For caste rules even the razor in India.

A little American girl, ill most of her life, was given five cents to buy an Easter egg. "Mother, do I *have* to spend this on candy?"

"No, dear. What would you like to buy?"

"I would like to send it to Dohnavur so the Lord Jesus can have another baby!"

One envelope with a check inside was addressed only "Dohnavur, India," arriving from China with thirteen different postmarks, four green seals, three purple registered stamps, plus messages and advice by kindly post office people scrawled around the edges. Since it was not addressed to any one person, or even to the Fellowship, it had to be returned. A long time later, it arrived properly addressed, very worn-looking, but the check inside was safe.

"Our ravens [crows] don't bring food; they snatch it out of our hands for themselves," objected a small girl hearing of Elijah for the first time.

"God's ravens are obedient," Amy assured her.

God never failed them, and by the end of the five-year war, all twelve nurseries were built and occupied, a wall a mile long was built, the forest property purchased and Forest House finished, not a child had gone hungry, and not a coolie had waited even a day for his pay.

The 1920s were years of marvelous growth. By 1923 there were twenty nurseries, and by 1924 twenty non-Indian workers belonged to the Fellowship. In 1927, a House of Prayer was built, and 1929 saw electricity installed and gifts earmarked "for X-ray equipment for the hospital," which they began to build that year. Over the years, a Ford car and ambulance were given.

"As thou hast believed, so be it done unto thee" (Matthew 8:13).

One more answer to prayer will have to represent the remainder of the years up to 1935. Amy never took the incoming funds for granted since she was living by faith, and faith grows stronger by testing. During World War I she had been offered a large garden just planted with orange, lime, and mango trees and had to refuse for lack of funds. In fact, the exchange of money almost threatened ruin to the work at the time. She kept praying. The land increased in value as the trees blossomed and bore fruit. In 1935 she was able to buy the garden plus adjoining fields for growing fodder for the animals. It was a long wait, but the field was much more valuable and she paid less.

"And they shall be mine, saith the Lord of Hosts, in that day when I make up my jewels."

Malachi 3:17

"Our Heavenly Father never takes any earthly thing from His children except He means to give them something better instead."

George Mueller

11
Crown Jewels

1900-1935, The Father's silence

"Why this waste?" Over and over the question came to Amy, her co-workers, to other Christians watching, who saw babies and children sicken and die after their rescue or saw other converts mature spiritually, then die just when they reached the point of being most usable. Was it all as water spilled on the ground?

A co-worker of Amy's traveled over 1,000 miles to save a baby boy who died a week later of diabetes. She had left on a Monday morning, traveled by bandy, bus, and train, changing twelve times before she reached Dohnavur late on Thursday. The best part of a week spent—for what?

"We never refuse a baby, and we can never stop hoping," Amy said. Children were lost by as little as a one-half hour delay. There was no time for questions such as "Was the mother healthy? Who was the father? Is the baby intelligent? What is the background?" Temple women did not ask questions, and they never refused a baby.

One three-day-old baby came as a complete surprise to Amy when the faithful Devai arrived in the middle of a night in a jingling bandy. Devai moved so quickly in the rescue that there hadn't been time to pray. The baby was beautiful with fair skin, and the mother had hidden her in a clay pot when Devai came to visit. "But earthen pots cannot hide from the eyes of the Lord," explained Devai, and she pleaded until God broke through caste and cruelty, and the mother finally said, "Let the Christians have the babe." She was healthy-looking but in a few days was gone from them.

Why? Amy could only try and gather comfort from the thought *She died with us and not with them.* "Given," she wrote the word alongside a date; then "taken," and another date. Her book was full of such recordings. "We live in the twilight of short knowledge," she wrote, and when one does not understand, one who trusts God is content to wait.

One of the merriest little persons who ever lived, Heart's Joy, starved to death because a special nutrient she took ran short, and the fresh supply was one day too late. "The torture of second causes is as the blackness of darkness," wrote Amy of that time.

Sometimes death was an answer to prayer. Death saved the child from sin. Lala was such a child. Five years old, with tiny hands and feet, elbows softly rounded like a conch shell, she was sent by friends to Dohnavur. Then her father, up to no good, demanded her back. Amy sent for a bandy, packed a bag of clothes for Lala, put a doll and a few candies into her hand, and parted with her.

Lala, gentle and trusting, would never be able to withstand pressure. Amy feared for her. She prayed that the child would either return safe to Dohnavur or be taken away from the evil her father planned for her.

Lala left in excellent health, but when she returned to the cold air of the hills she developed pneumonia. She died suddenly, after only a few days' illness. A pagan woman later meeting Amy told what she heard.

Lala said just before she died, "I am Jesus' child. I see three Shining Ones in my room. I am not afraid."

When the day came that Amy knew she must turn from ordinary missionary work to "carve a path through the jungle" of the secret trade in children, Ponnammal was her loyal stay. Ponnammal, too, saw the perishing children. A three-page official letter of criticism had come from England. Did they actually think Amy could stop praying that children be saved or refuse them when they were saved?

The three greatest losses of her life (after Walker *Iyer*, who died in 1912) were Ponnammal, her dearest companion in the faith; Arulai, whom she had trained to take over the women's work after she was gone; and Kohila, a young nurse whose wonderful rescue in childhood had foretold a great future for the Lord's work.

Ponnammal, her companion for eight years with the Starry Cluster, stood by her loyally. When Amy's health broke down it was Ponnammal who worked along in the Neyyoor nursery, through epidemics of smallpox and bacillary dysentery. "If another baby dies, we shall know the blessing of God is not on this work," said the only two women helping, and they prepared to leave.

Babies died, sometimes two in a day. Ponnammal was left with all the responsibility of mixing a different formula for each baby, besides the routine nursing. Can anyone who has had a sick, crying child in the home imagine what it was to have seventy such children all with fevers of 106°?

Just then two evil men who lived next to the nursery began to tempt the young convert girls and made Ponnammal's life a nightmare. Finally, after two and a half years at Neyyoor, Ponnammal returned to Dohnavur, bringing the babies. In her absence, a new nursery had been built. Still, apart from Mabel Wade, a trained nurse, they had no help and seldom enjoyed a full night's sleep. And this was the tropics! Amy sent letters to all the Christian pastors of South India: "Do you know of any Christian women who will help us, for love of God, living by faith?"

No such women exist anywhere in the church," the replies came back.

Amy and Ponnammal neared the breaking point again, worn by heat and worry, made worse every time Ponnammal left on a trip to save a child. She would return exhausted and weakened, her tiredness spilling out after hours in the noisy trains, sometimes traveling all night long in the aching, suffocating heat.

"Let us work until we drop," she told Amy, "but let us not lower our standards."

One Indian Christian who stayed with them a short time took care of the babies for six days, but when Sunday came, with her Bible under her arm she marched off to church leaving five screaming infants unfed, while a dozen others demanded diaper changes. "I go to do God's work," she said, as though the babies could be stored on shelves and left by themselves until Monday.

Other women stayed only a few days when they realized the work was "holy drudgery."

Ponnammal, being highly organized, took over

the baffling details connected with housekeeping in India, in addition to all her other work. Dohnavur was not near stores or market places. Rice, coconut, salt, sugar, oil, rope, and many other things must be purchased in quantity, after much haggling, all governed by petty, unreasonable laws and customs.

Her day began before dawn, after being up part of the night, when she mixed the food for the more delicate babies. "Oh, Lord, You know the insides of this little one. Guide my hand." More than one very sick child was brought back from the door of death because Ponnammal followed divine instruction rather than the directions on the label.

Five-thirty A.M. was prayer time with the convert girls who were learning to care for babies. Next, the milk sellers arrived, and she tested and measured milk, keeping a sharp eye open for trickery. One baby died two hours after drinking milk accidentally poisoned by a careless seller.

Medicines for ailing babies were worked out in great precision by Ponnammal as well as medicine for the village people who asked for help.

The only time she disagreed with Amy was over fresh air. Any Indian knew night air was poisonous, that it was best to board up every door and window at night. When her own daughter came home from boarding school with tubercular trouble, Ponnammal tried the open-air theory. Purripu recovered, grew strong and healthy, and Ponnammal no longer worried about the babies breathing night air.

Bible class with the young girls followed around noon, then an hour's rest in the hot part of the afternoon, provided there was no ill baby to claim her attention. Twilight, cow-dust time. The evening milk sellers reappeared, and the whole tiring routine must be patiently endured again.

Ponnammal had the ability to get workmen to work. One morning Amy eavesdropped and heard her bargaining with the head carpenter, a young man of weedy arms and legs.

"I cannot work without an advance of money," he said pitifully, lower lip drooping. "I have a large family." Heart-rending words, like oil wrung from the olive.

"Very well, I will pay you fifty annas now and fifty when the work is done."

The feather of a smile touched his eyes. He took the money and gulped water from a tin dipper. "O worthy one, I will begin as soon as I return from my grandmother's funeral."

"You gave that excuse last month!"

"Pardon, O speaker of truth. This is the *other* grandmother."

"Two months ago, you told me she—"

The carpenter made a polite little bow and prudently changed his story. "Pardon, I have forgotten. I must attend my niece's wedding *tamasha* (celebration). I will be back promptly, so speedily, knowing one, that you will never miss me."

Two weeks passed. No carpenter. Ponnammal paid three coolies to fan out and look for him in all the nearest villages. By the time he was found, the money that was to have been his wages had been paid to the coolies who found him.

He worked two full days in a row, taking only six naps. Then "O wise and discerning one, my elder brother's wife's sister has eaten a fever—"

Amy was more than glad to leave the hiring to Ponnammal.

Ponnammal shared Amy's attitude toward money; it had no power over her. God had authorized the work, so they looked to God alone. It was easier for them to have faith than to worry.

There was, however, anxiety about the continual additions to the family, especially after the death of Walker *Iyer*. He knew India as other Englishmen could not. His sympathy and wisdom had bolstered Amy's courage countless times. But how could they stop growing when God added to their number almost daily?

Seven months after Walker *Iyer's* death from ptomaine poisoning, Ponnammal was stricken down by cancer. For two years and five months she suffered. Operations, treatment, and medicine gave only temporary relief.

The aspirin supply ran out one day in May in the worst of the hot season when the other workers were taking a much-needed rest at the Forest House high in the mountains. Amy substituted another medicine, which proved worthless. She wired immediately to a supply place, but five long days passed before it arrived. Ponnammal was without medicine in the last stages of cancer. She lay in torment, not even able to speak. Afterward, she described the experience. "When the pain was at its worst the Lord Himself stood by me and set a boundary for the pain."

She dreamed one night that she was sinking in a river, snagged in weeds. When she called out, instantly the Lord Himself lifted her, and she began to sing praise and hosannas along with a heavenly choir.

She soon needed larger doses of drugs, as the

pain increased. During her last weeks her room was kept darkened and quiet. Three of the noisiest, most active little tots—Tara, Evu, and Lullitha—came one at a time and sat for an hour in perfect silence by Ponnammal's bed, such was the peace that reigned in the room.

One day Ponnammal's father and the village barber visited. "How long has she to live?" demanded the old father in a loud voice.

Ponnammal's sense of humor rose above her pain, and she burst out laughing.

The two men stared. They had never seen a dying person who had no fear. The barber was most disapproving. The proper treatment, in his opinion, would have been a poultice of wild pig tusk, rhinoceros horn, tiger claw, and a little pulverized silver. Ponnammal spoke a few words of the One in Whom she had confidence, but the words were unnecessary. The men had seen "the sermon written in her face."

On August 26, 1915, it was night on earth, but for Ponnammal it was day. And the night was filled with voices singing, "Her warfare is accomplished."

Arulai was ten years old when she first heard of a God who could change a person's disposition. She was a child with a bad temper who often prayed, "Great Siva, change me."

Nature was smiling that day, an azure sky overhead, when Arulai on her way to draw water heard Walker *Iyer* preaching by the roadside. "There is a living God! He turned me, a lion, into a lamb!" he cried, and Arulai stopped dead. Who could he mean? Listening further she heard of

Jesus Lord, then she noticed Amy in Indian dress. She felt strongly drawn to her.

"If only she knew how much I want to learn about the living God she would ask me to live with her and be her little girl."

Arulai eventually was permitted to stay with Amy, and after much personal suffering caused by family problems and the loss of Supu, whom she might have married, Arulai traveled with Amy.

Arulai's name meant Star of Grace. Stars shine forever. Arulai never looked back or regretted, once she set her hand to the plow. God's grace kept her steady.

When she was only fifteen years old she spoke to an audience of thousands of people at a gathering of the Syrian Church in South India. Forty years of service were poured out upon the children's work, and Amy felt sure Arulai was to be the leader of the women after her own passing. It was not to be.

Arulai fell ill in 1935, and though she was able to translate a few of Amy's books into Tamil, she could not leave her bed.

Amy called May 24, 1936, "Arulai's Celestial Birthday." There was no other Indian Christian woman to take Arulai's place, and Amy had been looking forward to Indian leadership. And she was gone. But Amy had to remember Dohnavur was built by God.

Satan seemed to say, "You see, you have had to fall back."

Amy replied, "Then we fall back upon God."

In December 1942, four-year-old Kohila, described by Amy as "a small brown Skye terrier with curls," arrived at Dohnavur after some frightening experiences. A few days of love and petting made a difference, and she settled easily into nursery life with 200 other children. The spiritual training of another child for soldiership began.

Kohila went with Amy and the other children to sing in nearby villages and helped distribute Bible verse cards. A few weeks later her guardians demanded her return. When Amy refused to send the child back to the destruction waiting for her, they brought a criminal case against Amy.

Amy called the workers together and said bluntly, "I really do not expect to be with you a week from now." A conviction of the kidnapping charge meant seven years' imprisonment. A faithful worker at Dohnavur, Arul Dasan, offered to help "disappear" Kohila and hurriedly took her hundreds of miles away to missionaries who sheltered her for the next five months.

The law of the land was good, it deterred crime, but Amy knew the law had not been framed with the knowledge of children in moral danger. No laws existed at all for *their* protection. She recognized a higher Law against which she dared not sin.

Amy was sure they all faced prison because of little Kohila's case. But, "There arose a great storm . . . and he arose" (Mark 4:37,39). The very day after she wrote those words, a telegram arrived. "Criminal case dismissed."

Kohila grew up and became a schoolgirl. Lessons did not come easy to her, but she studied hard until she mastered every difficulty. She accepted Christ as Savior when she was eleven.

When she was seventeen she became an *accal* in the nursery prior to training as a hospital nurse.

"Next to helping people, what do you think was her greatest pleasure?" Amy asked a friend of Kohila's.

"I think it was singing."

Kohila became head nurse at Dohnavur. "Love for others was her last thought," wrote a *sittie* who worked with her. Kohila always took on the difficult cases or offered to work with a difficult nurse. Kohila always volunteered to miss the treat, if a substitute was needed.

Kohila had set her heart on gathering purple flowers to decorate another nurse's room on her Coming Day, and she hiked up a mountain ravine and climbed a steep rock slope. Halfway up, her foot slipped, and she fell headlong. Shortly after the accident, she died.

A faithful head nurse gone. An overworked, short-handed hospital staff. "Carried by angels," was all Amy had the heart to write in her diary, alongside the date.

Gone, four of the finest—Walker *Iyer*, Ponnammal, Arulai, Kohila. There could be no futile crying of "Why?" for Amy. She had learned to accept the silence of God.

"He shall sit like a refiner and purifier of silver."

Malachi 3:3

"How very beautiful these gems are! It is strange how deeply colors seem to penetrate one like scent. I suppose that is the reason why gems are used as spiritual emblems in Revelations. They look like fragments of heaven."

George Eliot

12
The Jeweler

1931-1951, The Father's plan

God works with souls like a jeweler works with gems. Once He finds and brings them to the Light, they are cut, polished, and placed in a setting of His choice.

In the natural state, diamonds appear as hard, irregular lumps that shine only with a greasy luster and not all with their finished brilliance. Their beauty is given them by the skill of the stonecutter, who grinds and polishes their surfaces so that they sparkle.

Not the size of a diamond, but the light reflected gives the stone its value. The Tiffany diamond, now valued at $2,000,000, was cut from 287.42 carets to 128.5l carets, with 90 facets, making it into a gemmy sun. When displayed in the Fifth Avenue store window it could be seen all the way across the avenue.

The only way the value of a diamond can be increased is by cutting. Experts in Paris studied the Tiffany diamond for one year before a single blow was struck in the cutting.

In the cutting of the Regent diamond, the most treasured of the French crown jewels, size was sacrificed for brilliancy. The standard fifty-eight facet cut sets off this most brilliant of stones, but the size decreased from 410 carets to 140.5 carets.

Diamond—crystalized carbon, the hardest substance in existence. It has been through the fire. The diamonds that reflect the most light have received the roughest treatment. Yet the greatest care is taken by the jeweler not to damage the stone in any way. Every flaw must be cut out, even a microscopic flaw.

From 1901 to 1931, Amy had been active and in "spare" time wrote twenty-two books. Then, in September 1931, she went to the Hindu town of Kalakadu, about four miles north of Dohnavur, to inspect a house called haunted, which was offered to them as an outpost for some of their workers. In her quiet time with the Lord that morning she had prayed, "Do with me as Thou wilt. *Do anything,* Lord, that will fit me to serve Thee and help my beloveds."

That evening, while walking around the house at Kalakadu, God began to answer her prayer. She slipped and fell into a pit dug by coolies in the wrong spot. Her leg was broken, and her ankle dislocated. Acute neuritis later disabled one arm. Arthritic pain of the spine set in, and for twenty years she rarely left her room and was never without pain. Another fall in her room broke her hip and arm. The last two years of her life she could not get out of bed. The slightest moving was almost impossible, and drugs no longer controlled the constant pain.

Answered prayer? Amy had prayed, "*Do anything,* Lord." And He continued to facet the diamond.

Her family, who had been used to seeing her hurry about her work like a hare, found it hard to accept the situation. Amy was still active, but her activity was confined to one room, and it was activity of the inner life.

"I think it is true to say that God used her pen for more widespread and deeper spiritual blessing during the post-accident period than in all the preceding years," wrote Bishop Frank Houghton, an earlier biographer.

Her two books written "by the ill to the ill," *Rose From Briar* and *Gold by Moonlight,* are classics in their field. In them she points out that God, our captain, does not shelve His soldiers as though they were cracked pottery. Soldiers are simply assigned to other tasks, some to suffer for His sake, some to wage war in a field of prayer.

Thirteen books were written after her accident, making a total of thirty-five. Her books were never "popular" in the sense that popular books are easy to read, titillating to the senses, with happy predictable endings. When she first saw them described in a catalogue as "popular," "she was horrified. Popular? The books were written on a battlefield—are they being read only to satisfy curiosity and titillate imagination? She prayed that every book and letter that was sent out from Dohnavur would have blood and iron in it. Some people speak of 'enjoying' missions. Would they 'enjoy' watching a shipwreck?"

It was not easy to find publishers who would publish the truth. Amy never asked what the public wanted.

There were days when she worked on her writing thirteen hours straight, sometimes after sleepless nights. The "fellowship of His suffering" gave her later books great depth and beauty. Twelve of the books were put into Braille in England and eight for the Braille Circulating Library in the United States.

Always a lover of good books, Amy found plenty

of time to read. She was familiar not only with the church Fathers and pioneers of all ages and nationalities, and great literature of all countries, but also with the Tamil authors and other Hindu literature.

She wrote poems and songs for her family, many of which were set to music.

"Which is harder?" she asked herself during those twenty years of confinement. "To be well and doing things? Or, to be ill and bearing things?" To fret and demand healing was foreign to her. Nor did she think of illness as a punishment for sin for a Christian who was walking in the light. Yet she longed to be done with weakness and pain forever.

Always observant and artistic, her love of color and nature appear in all her books. Nothing was too small to be noticed. Her sharp eye once saw and described in botanist's language a miniature fugus, pale gold, with rings of deepening brown and fluted edges. She compared the pattern to that of a moth's wing and found to her delight that they matched. Carefully she recorded the descriptions for the pleasure of the children.

For six years Amy had prayed for a house to rent in the Brahmin town of Kalakadu, and the prayer was finally answered. Then she prayed for just the right Christian man to live there and be a witness. The day she received the key to the house (the day of her fall), an old man, worn with travel, asked to spend the night at Dohnavur. The next day he told them he was a Christian, a Brahmin. His name was Triumph.

For seven years he had searched for peace, studying with a famous guru of Benares. One day he found the guru with an open Bible in his lap, reading the fourteenth chapter of John, tears streaming down his cheeks.

The guru turned to his pupil. "Have you found peace the seven years you read the Vedas?"

"No," Triumph replied.

"You will never find it there," said the guru. "I have found peace in the gospel of Jesus Christ, but I am afraid to confess Him before men."

For many months the two men, teacher and pupil, read together from the Bible until the scales fell completely from their eyes. God led Triumph to travel until he stopped overnight at Dohnavur.

Surely he is the answer to our prayer, thought Amy. She gave him the key to the house in Kalakadu, and he lived there a few months. Then diabetes seized him, the dry heat making him worse. He was subject to delusions and could no longer witness. He returned to his own town, and Kalakadu was left without a witness.

Months passed, and a sick man was brought in to the Dohnavur hospital from Kalakadu. He told how he had been won to Christ by Triumph. *Surely the answer to our prayer this time,* Amy thought.

Before he could even begin a ministry, a mind-destroying drug was slipped into his drink, and he went mad. The recovery room of the hospital was only fifty yards from Amy's room, and she could hear his terrible cries night and day, like "the powers of darkness shouting in triumph." At last the noise stopped; the man was dead.

Amy had prayed that God would enable her to do more for her family—then the fall into the pit. She prayed six years for a convert to work in Kalakadu—then came the disabling of the only man who could have done this. A convert from Kalakadu was finally found—then came his death.

She ran from the thought that the Father did anything that needed to be explained. "Faith never wonders why," she often quoted, and now she was called upon to practice what she told others.

One day Amy asked the nurse who cared for her what were the chief trials of sick people. "Monotony; the same room, the same routine, the same food, the same faces, the same sounds, the same pain." And Amy remembered the Lord Jesus Christ hanging helpless on His cross, when a day seemed as a thousand. "In all points tempted like as we are" (Hebrews 4:15). She often read this verse and commented: "Unrecorded experiences of suffering lie there."

Thousands of years ago there was a battle fought whose outcome was determined by the prayer of one who could not fight, but could only lift his hands in prayer (Exodus 17:8-16). Victory was given by God, not because of valiant soldiers, excellent weapons, nourishing food and drink, or favoring weather, but because of one who prayed.

The priesthood of the believer had always been active in Amy's life, but now she could give herself to it unreservedly. Prayer provides laborers for the harvest, the Bible teaches (Matthew 9:37-38), and more and more workers were added to Dohnavur as Amy prayed. Prayer throws light on the problem of pointless pain. Some Scripture can be understood only by identical experience with it.

On one of her worst days, Amy imagined the Lord's saying to her, "It is finished." Though aching to hear such words, she borrowed a few lines from an old poem and told of the regret that would flood her soul.

"Thou wouldst say, 'So soon?
Let me go back and suffer yet a while
More patiently; I have not yet praised God.' "

To the very end, on January 18, 1951, the radiating diamond that was her life reflected the Light that lights the world.

Significant Dates

1867 Amy born in Millisle, Ireland

1879 Attends Wesleyan boarding school

1883 Her conversion

1884 Works in street missions

1886 Spiritual crisis in meeting in Scotland where she hears Jude 24

1889 Moves to England; does slum work in Manchester

1890 Moves to Broughton Grange

1892 Call to mission field

1893-1894 Term of service in Japan

1895 Arrives in India (Madras and Bangalore)

1896-1898 Moves to Tinnevelly District (villages of Palamcottah and Pannaivilai); works with Starry Cluster

1899 Jewel of Victory and Jewel of Life escape to Amy; Arulai converted; Pearleyes escapes to Amy

1900 Moves to Dohnavur

1903 *Things As They Are* published; the Walkers return to England

1904 Sixteen child converts; six children saved from temples

1905 The celebration of "Coming Days" begun; death of babies Amethyst and Sapphire; Amy's mother visits; death of Robert Wilson

1906 Epidemic of cholera in village of Dohnavur

1907 Mable Wade, first European, arrives to

help; first gift of £200 to build nurseries

1908 Ponnammal returns from Neyyoor Nursery to Dohnavur

1909 Muttammal escapes

1911 Amy and workers face imprisonment because of Muttammal

1912 Walker *Iyer* dies

1913 Family numbers 130; Kohila rescued; more land purchased

1915 Ponnammal dies

1916 Sisters of the Common Life founded

1917 Grey Jungle land purchased; Forest House built

1918 First baby boy accepted; rescue work for boys begun

1919 Great financial problems and testing; Kaiser-i-Hind Medal for service to the people of India offered to Amy; refuses, later accepts out of politeness.

1923 Twenty nurseries in Dohnavur

1924 Dr. May Powell arrives to stay

1926 Dr. Godfrey Webb-Peploe arrives to stay; eighty baby boys rescued

1927 £100 given to begin building hospital; House of Prayer built

1928 Dr. Murray Webb-Peploe arrives to stay; land purchased for boys' work

1929 Electricity and X-ray equipment installed at Dohnavur

1931 Amy's accident

1936 Arulai dies

1947 *Things As They Are* reprinted for thirteenth time

1951 Amy dies

1952 Family numbers over nine hundred

Glossary

aiyo alas!

ander inner, hidden room of house

accal older sister

amma mother

avatar a religious leader, a god incarnation

batooras rooms in which to store fuel cakes

buthil substitute

camasu small girl's dress

chirag lamp of clay dish for oil and wick

caravanserai inn

dharma duty

dhoti a man's wear of long strip of cloth
    wrapped around torso

devadasi a servant of the gods, dancing girl,
    temple prostitute

ghat a platform for cremation

ghee butter boiled and skimmed

grabha-griha womb house in temple, the inner
    shrine

himsa torture in prison to secure a confession

Iyer ordained pastor, teacher

Jorabodha ceremony of awakening the god

karma law of cause and effect

mantra the name of a Hindu demon used in
    meditation

monsoon rainy season ushered in by wind

mudra hand gestures in a dance

nirvana state of nothingness, union with a god

Put hell

putra Sanskrit word for son, meaning "deliverer from hell"

pyre woodpile for burning a dead body

rupee worth 20¢; sixteen rupees = 1 English pound; one rupee = 16 annas; one anna = 12 pies

sari Indian woman's dress

suttee voluntary cremation; word originally meant "faithful wife"

sunnyasin Indian religious beggar

tamasha celebration

yupa sacrificial post in temple, where animals were slaughtered

zenana harem

Sources

Houghton, Frank. *Amy Carmichael of Dohnavur*. London: SPCK, 1953.

By Amy Carmichael:

Gold Cord. Fort Washington, Pa.: Christian Literature Crusade, 1957.
His Thoughts Said. London: SPCK, 1958.
If. Dohnavur, India: Dohnavur Fellowship, 1938.
Kohila. London: SPCK, 1963.
Lotus Buds. London: SPCK, 1909.
Mimosa. Dohnavur, India: Dohnavur Fellowship, n.d.
Nor Scrip. London: SPCK, 1950.
Ploughed Under. London: SPCK, 1953.
Rose from Briar. London: SPCK, 1957.
Tables in the Wilderness. London: SPCK, 1923.
Though Mountains Shake. New York: Loizeaux, 1946.
Thou Givest. Dohnavur, India: Dohnavur Fellowship, 1958.

Moody Press, a ministry of the Moody Bible Institute, is designed for education, evangelization, and edification. If we may assist you in knowing more about Christ and the Christian life, please write us without obligation: Moody Press, c/o MLM, Chicago, IL 60610.